Brooklyn Baby

A Hollywood Star's Amazing Journey Through Love, Loss & Laughter

Joan Steiger
& David Minasian

Albany, Georgia

Brooklyn Baby: A Hollywood Star's Amazing Journey Through Love, Loss & Laughter
Copyright © 2016 Joan Steiger & David Minasian. All Rights Reserved.

No part of this book may be reproduced in any form or by any means, electronic, mechanical, digital, photocopying or recording, except for the inclusion in a review, without permission in writing from the the publisher.

Published in the USA by
BearManor Media
P.O. Box 71426
Albany, GA 31708
www.BearManorMedia.com

Softcover Edition
ISBN-10: 1593939140
ISBN-13: 978-1-59393-914-4

Printed in the United States of America

Table of Contents

Prologue: Stranger Than Fiction — vii

Chapter 1: You Make Me Feel Like Dancing — 1
Chapter 2: To Rome With Love — 9
Chapter 3: The Mystery Of The Chelsea Hotel — 19
Chapter 4: California Dreamin' — 25
Chapter 5: This Could Be The Start Of Something Big — 29
Chapter 6: Indecent Proposals — 39
Chapter 7: The Hills Are Alive — 53
Chapter 8: The Wild Wild West — 77
Chapter 9: The King & Queen of Sunset Plaza — 93
Chapter 10: Party Central — 107
Chapter 11: In The Heat Of The Moment — 121
Chapter 12: The End Of An Era — 139
Chapter 13: Riding With Angels — 173
Chapter 14: My Heart Will Go On — 193

Epilogue: Mischievous — 203
Index — 207

Prologue
Stranger Than Fiction

For me, real life is indeed stranger than fiction. I remember on one occasion, Jack Lemmon sat at the grand piano in our living room playing an impromptu jazz piece. It sounded great! He looked up momentarily from the keyboard and smiled over in our direction. My good friend Don Knotts and I were sitting on the sofa, reminiscing over some of the behind-the-scenes shenanigans that had gone on during the filming of *The Prizefighter* a few years earlier. I glanced over at the lovely antique clock that had been in my family ever since I could remember. It was 3 a.m.

When Jack had finished playing, the three of us made our way out to the patio where the insanity had kicked into high gear. We slid open the glass door and were instantly immersed in a sea of laughter that had become commonplace at our large, semi-annual parties. The combined comedic talents of Jonathan Winters and my late husband John Myhers had everyone in stitches.

Soon, we were all laughing so hard, we actually had to call out, "Enough!" Alcohol had been flowing freely for several hours, and while that may have helped contribute to the riotous atmosphere, it was nevertheless a well known fact that these were two of the funniest people on the planet. Once again, everyone was having the time of their lives. I felt lucky to be counted among such wonderful friends.

The view of Hollywood from our Sunset Plaza home circa 1966

I remember it being exceptionally clear that night. From the garden of our Sunset Plaza home you could see all of Hollywood. And by the time we said our goodbyes to the last of the guests, the sun was just moments away from making an appearance on the horizon.

Rod Steiger

Years later, my new beau Rod Steiger asked me to accompany him to the 70th annual Academy Awards ceremony. Normally he didn't like going to these types of events, but he knew I hadn't been before and thought it would be a treat for me. The Academy was paying special tribute to past best actor and actress winners and had requested that he attend.

Rod's award winning performance from In The Heat Of The Night

Rod of course had won the Oscar in 1967 for his portrayal of police chief Bill Gillespie in the classic film *In the Heat of the Night*, winning over fellow nominees Warren Beatty, Dustin Hoffman, Paul Newman, and Spencer Tracy—formidable opponents indeed. From my vantage point in the audience near the front of the Shrine Auditorium, I watched as each of the past winners was introduced in alphabetical order. There was my Rod on stage, sandwiched between Mira Sorvino and Shirley Temple.

Rod Steiger (front row, center) at the Academy Awards

Earlier in the month, Elizabeth Taylor had asked if Rod would be so kind as to escort her to the awards show. He declined, politely informing her that he would be taking me instead. Not one to take no for an answer, Liz suggested he take both of us—to which Rod firmly replied that there was no way that was going to happen. This event would trigger a series of notorious tabloid stories that would haunt the three of us over the next few years.

Once married, Rod and I decided to travel around the world as part of an extended honeymoon and wound up in San Francisco. We were waiting in the crowded lobby, about to check into the Clift Hotel, when suddenly we heard a voice cry out, "Rod! Rod!" We turned around in time to see Robin Williams running toward us. He and Rod had never met before. Robin pleaded with us, "You have to come over for dinner. I'll pick you up myself." Of course we agreed. The next night he came to get us in his SUV and took us to his home

> # Rod and Liz: Just Pals
> "Elizabeth Taylor and I are just good friends," insisted Rod Steiger, 74. There has been gossip about the two Oscar-winners spending time together, but Steiger told us he already has "a lady friend"—Joan Benedict, who was on *General Hospital*.
> Liz credited Steiger with helping her get back out in the world after a fall in February 1998.

The tabloids having a field day with Rod and me

in Tiberon, the same house where years later his assistant Rebecca Spencer would find his lifeless body.

We had a lovely, intimate evening. Robin was funny, but wasn't "on" like he was when performing. He really wanted to meet Rod and loved him so much. In retrospect, I believe their connection was likely due to their common battle with depression. Robin was aware of Rod's history and soon after that initial meeting, the two of them would occasionally get together to share their experiences.

By the fall of 2004, I was starring in a provocative play written by noted playwright Donald Marguiles called *Collected Stories* which chronicled the disintegrating relationship between a young writer and her mentor. There was a line in the script where my character Ruth recalled how the aroma from the Italian restaurant she lived above would always manage to seep its way into her apartment.

Each night during the performance, that line would immediately snap me back to my childhood in Brooklyn. I grew up in my grandfather's four story brownstone near Prospect Park. Cooking was my grandfather's hobby, and the heavenly scent of his never ending Italian dishes would permeate the house.

It was an unusual childhood to say the least: Living in a mansion with seven uncles, performing my first dance recital at the Brooklyn Academy of Music at age seven, and being shipped off by myself to live in Rome at the age of ten. Little did I know at the time that I was being prepared for an amazing roller coaster ride—filled to the brim with some of the most incredible highs and darkest lows that the entertainment business and life in general have to offer.

So how did this *Brooklyn Baby* end up on the inside of Hollywood's inner circle? I do remember the day I told my mother I wanted to be an actress. Ever since I was little, she had always encouraged me to develop my talent, and my father's reaction was what any teenager dreaming of stardom could have hoped for. "We'll find you the best schools, the best teachers and the best agents," he promised. And he did just that, making arrangements for me in New York while I finished up my final semester of high school. With graduation only a few weeks away, I couldn't wait to get started. The future was looking very bright indeed.

And then my mother received the call . . .

The voice on the other end told her that there had been a terrible accident at the historic Chelsea Hotel in Manhattan where my father had been staying. The news caught us totally off guard. I was beyond devastated. How could this have happened? What exactly had transpired in that hotel room? For some reason the police were being vague. Was it simply an accident or something far more sinister? I was determined to find out.

This would mark the first time in my life that a man I dearly loved would be taken from me.

And it wouldn't be the last . . .

Chapter 1

You Make Me Feel Like Dancing

IT WAS MY GRANDFATHER'S DREAM to be like Aristotle Onassis and, just like the Greek tycoon, my grandfather had become very successful in the shipping business. Hailing from a much different era than today, my grandfather had been sent over to America from his native Italy by his parents due to being illegitimate. My grandmother, who was also of Italian descent, had come from a lovely upper class family in Naples. Together they had ten children, which included my mother, two aunts and seven uncles. Even after the children were grown, they all continued to live in the same house in an exclusive neighborhood in Brooklyn. Imagine that! This was the house I grew up in.

And what a house it was! My grandfather had lots of money and owned a four story brownstone on 7th Street, just two doors down from Prospect Park. Most of the houses on the street were mansions and ours was one of the nicest. It was all very beautiful, elegant and quiet. Many of the families in the neighborhood were Irish. We were the only Italians.

Besides his love of cooking, which created a heavenly scent throughout the house on a daily basis, my grandfather was fond of playing solitaire. He would usually cheat at it—which never really made sense to me. Dinner was promptly served at six every night and we were all required to be present. There was a dumb waiter and an intercom system throughout the house, along with an exquisite sitting room complete with a beautiful grand piano that had special rolls of music you could insert into it, like a player piano. I loved it! In fact, the 7th Street house always had something going on. It was a life unto itself, filled with all kinds of magical activities. Many years later, my husband Rod and I drove past it while visiting New York and discovered that the property had undergone a historical restoration causing its value to skyrocket past $18 million!

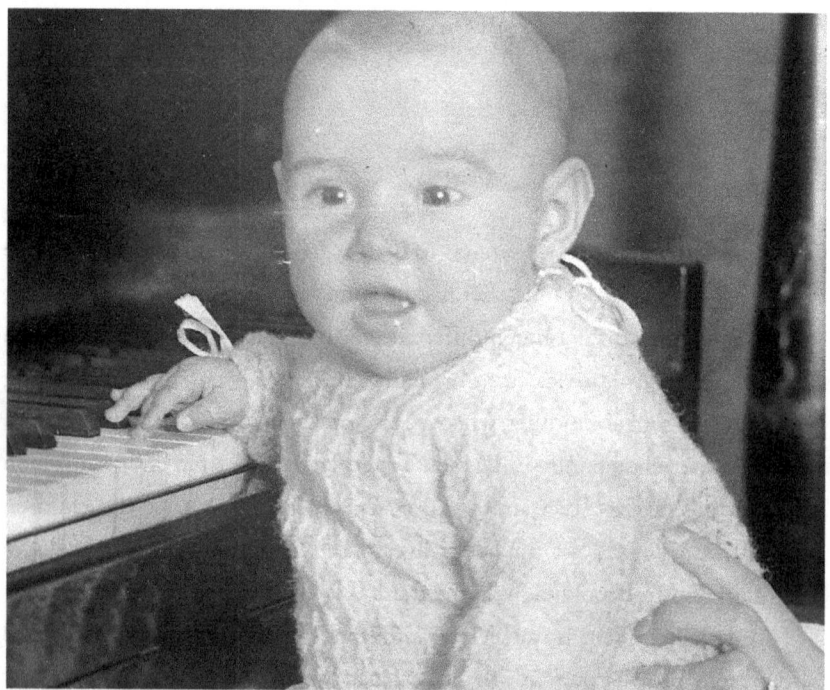

That's me, camera ready from the start

I was born at the huge New York Methodist Hospital which was literally a block away from the house. I was the first grandchild and, for a while, the only child living in our gigantic mansion. It was an unusual childhood to say the least, being surrounded by all these uncles. Each one was unique. One was a well known photographer for the *New York Daily News* who provided me with my first ever publicity photo when I was appearing in the play *Dr. Faustus*. Another worked for the *Washington Post* and still another helped in the development of stereophonic sound. I was later told by his daughter that this third uncle was also with the CIA. These uncles gave me lots of attention and helped to raise me, since my father was rarely around.

My uncle Pat, photographer for the New York Daily News, *second from left*

One incident that had a tremendous impact on my life occurred on my first day of kindergarten. The principal took one look at me and announced, "You look like such a smart girl. Why don't we move you up to the first grade?" Strangely, I hadn't even been tested yet, so how could he know? That one event has stayed with me my whole life, and it provided me with a sense of confidence at a very young age. As a result, I've learned that whatever you say to a child, whether it be good or bad, can have an effect on them for the rest of their lives.

These were elegant times. One of my aunts would dress me up and take me across the street to Prospect Park every afternoon to watch the lawn tennis matches. She would also take me to the Botanical Gardens. I recall seeing the Good Humor man come around every day at 4 p.m., and I would always say "hi" to Tony the iceman. In many ways I felt like Eloise from the classic *Eloise at the Plaza* book series by Kay Thompson. The books followed the escapades of a precocious six year old girl who lived at the Plaza Hotel in New York and viewed the hotel as her playhouse. To me, there wasn't much difference between Eloise and me, or between my big house and the Plaza Hotel.

As a child, I didn't have a lot of playmates, but it didn't bother me. I did have one friend named Susan. I remember she had a Shirley Temple doll which my mother wasn't too keen on (she didn't like Shirley Temple's curls). I think I compensated for the lack of friends by developing a very active imagination, which in turn probably triggered my eventual love of acting. I actually enjoyed the solitude and never felt lonely. I always found something to do. I was usually too excited to take naps, so I never took them (I still don't). Early on, I developed a very positive outlook and a real love for life, regardless of the circumstances . . . a trait which has endured a lifetime.

One afternoon, the doorbell rang. My mother found a package addressed to me sitting by the doorstep. Inside was an expensive diamond ring along with a note in child's writing that said, "I love you, Joanie . . . signed Robert." It turned out that a classmate of mine named Robert had "borrowed" his grandmother's diamond ring from atop her dresser and given it to me as a gift. Of course, we returned it right away. But I must say that this was a great experience for a young girl. My sensibilities told me that boys were wonderful and fun . . . a feeling that I've held to this day!

The first movie I ever saw was *Top Hat* starring Ginger Rogers and Fred Astaire. I was seven years old at the time and I knew this was it! I was certain that I wanted to become a dancer. Soon thereafter, I started tap lessons, and then ballet. I thought Shirley Temple was a great tap dancer

(which worried my mother, you know, the curls) but Eleanor Powell was definitely the best. She was the only person I knew who could do cartwheels while dancing! Ginger Rogers was wonderful, and a good actress too. Ruby Keeler was the funniest of all the dancers. And how did Ann Miller manage to never get dizzy? I remember my first dance teacher was named Daisy and my first recital was at the Brooklyn Academy of Music. Although my mother dutifully arranged for me to take lessons and make all my costumes, she never once came to any of my performances.

Like my mother, my father also came from a big family—a family of seven. All the other girls at school thought he was so handsome … and he was! He was quite the ladies man too. He frequently cheated on my mother. He wasn't like other fathers that I knew … he drank a lot and was a gambler. Still, I thought he was terrific. They called him Cy, which was short for cyclone. I actually spent more time with my uncles than my father since he was rarely home. One time, he broke down in front of me, crying, and confessed that he wasn't a good father. I tried to tell him "no," but we both knew it was true. And even though he didn't set a good example, I still loved him very much.

If I saw something I liked, my father would always buy it for me. He bought lots of things for himself, too. Every year he would get himself a new car, and always seemed to be waxing it. He had a real need for speed and usually drove well over the limit. I seemed to have inherited that particular trait from him. He became a championship boxer while in the Marines. One time when I was very young, he took me to Jones Beach on Long Island and into the Atlantic. To him it was fun and exciting. But to me it was a terrifying experience. I've been afraid of the ocean ever since.

And always, in the back of my mind, I knew someway, somehow, he would meet an untimely death.

My mother was ahead of her time. She would take me to museums, which I loved. However, she was not very affectionate. I don't recall her ever kissing me. Being Italian you would think it would be a natural thing, but for her, it wasn't. I'm very affectionate, but I never saw my parents show any kind of affection toward each other. In fact, it was quite the opposite. We lived in this beautiful house which was marred only by their constant arguing. Hearing them always fight made me a nervous wreck. I couldn't stand it. As a result, I vowed never to argue with my spouse when I got older. Frankly, my parents were not suited for each other, and it was only a matter of time before they separated.

My mother in later years

St. Savior's Elementary School, which is now a high school

I attended St. Savior's Catholic School on 6th Street in Brooklyn, which was just around the corner from our house. I still remember the nuns there at the school. I was never that good of a student, and I hated math. But what I did like was the boys. I was boy crazy! I still am! I also loved going to church, mostly for the singing. I loved to sing. I frequently get asked if I'm a singer and I always say, "No, Barbra Streisand is a singer." I attended St. Savior's until the age of ten.

Me with my Father and younger brother

Then one day, out of the blue, my mother announced that she was sending me to Rome . . .

Chapter 2

To Rome With Love

I wasn't scared. I saw it as some kind of adventure. Here I was at the ripe old age of ten being shipped off by my mom to Italy, by myself, to live with a group of people I had never met. Most kids that age would have been petrified. Not me. I was thinking to myself that this could be fun.

Without my knowledge, my mother had called up her cousins in Rome and arranged for me to come live with them. I'm not really sure exactly why my mother believed this was a good idea. By now I had already been dancing for three years and perhaps she thought Italy would be a wonderful place for me to continue my training. Or maybe she just wanted to protect me from the constant bickering between her and my father. In any event, from that moment on, things would be very different.

I recall my mother putting me on this huge ship, and in no time I was sailing across the Atlantic toward Europe. At first, I didn't know a single soul on board. But soon I was befriended by a very nice woman who also happened to be traveling from New York to Rome. As it turned out, she was the secretary to Robert Ripley, the man who had become famous for creating the *Ripley's Believe It Or Not* newspaper columns, radio shows and television programs.

I suppose I should have been traumatized. But I actually found the whole thing to be rather exciting. Over the years, a few people have asked me if I was simply born with courage or if it was something I learned. It's really hard to say. I think it comes down to a person's spirit. We all have choices to make. Ever since I can remember, I've been filled with a zest for life, and I'm able to easily adapt to just about any situation.

To my delight, upon my arrival in Rome, I was welcomed with open arms. My mother's cousins, simply put, were wonderful people. Everyone spoke Italian, and I didn't. But I quickly learned. I had a private tutor named Yole Yolie (who could forget that name?) and within a week, I could converse with my relatives. For me, learning a new language at that age was an easy task. The house where I would now be living was magnificent. It was a fifteen room villa with a live-in maid! At night you would leave your shoes outside the door of your room and in the morning they would be shined, ready to go. They even had a chapel inside the house where you could go and pray.

My mother was very avant-garde in her thinking and had always been great when it came to teaching me about culture. Prior to my arrival in Italy, she had arranged to have me enrolled in the prestigious Rome Opera Ballet School where I would now be studying dance. My ballet teacher was the famous Madame Battaggia. But within a week, I knew I wanted to be a tap dancer rather than a ballerina due to the grueling work that was required.

My mother had always tried to encourage me to sing in addition to studying dance. In fact, her cousin was Pasquale Di Costanzo, impresario of the famous opera house in Naples. So, I was asked if I also wanted to become an opera singer. There were discussions about enrolling me in opera classes while in Rome, but my passion really was dancing. Every evening, all of the relatives in the house would play music and I would dance. It was a magical time.

All of my school lessons were privately tutored and, again, I didn't have any playmates. During my free time, I would roller skate by myself all over the hills of Rome. One time I recall wanting to fix the hair and nails of Pierina, the family maid. She seemed game. So I gathered up all my supplies and got to work. I thought it would be fun to make her look pretty. When my relatives found out however, they quickly put a stop to it. Apparently, I had crossed a cultural boundary. Interacting with the maid on that level just wasn't something you were supposed to do back then, which made me quite sad.

Before coming to Italy, I would be so stressed at night in my room in New York listening to my parents argue, that I would often wake up the next morning to find that I had wet the bed. But the minute I got away from my parents and arrived in Rome, the bed wetting instantly stopped, never to return. The stress was now gone.

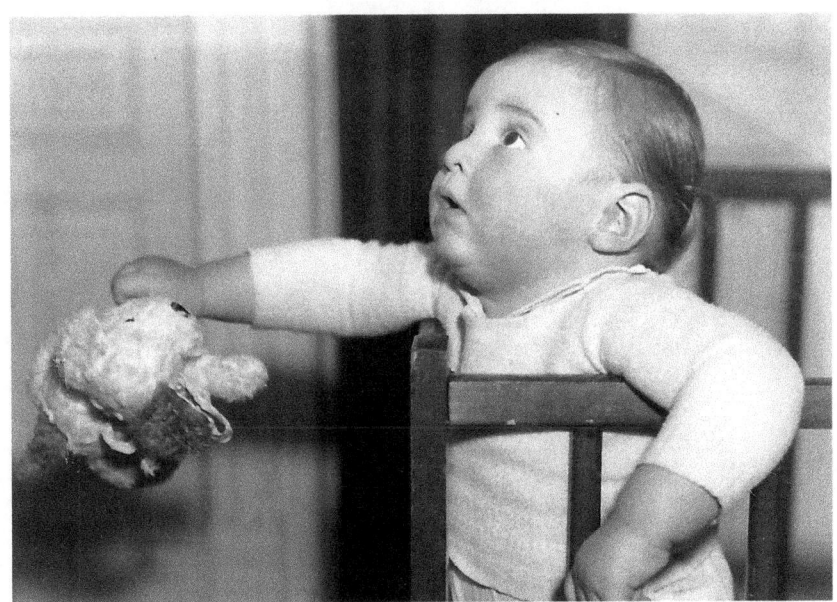

My baby brother "Gene"

As soon as the school year was over, my mother and younger brother Gene arrived to take me home (his real name was George, but we all called him Gene. He was strikingly handsome and grew up to be an amazing athlete). So I packed up all my things. But before we left, we had one final night of music at the villa with all the other relatives. As I was preparing to dance, I saw my mother suddenly walk over to the piano, sit down and begin to play! I was stunned. I had no idea she knew piano. And she played beautifully. That was the first—and only—time I ever heard her play.

My handsome brother George "Gene" Benedict, all grown up

Now instead of going straight back to New York, the three of us traveled to Paris and remained there for a year. My mother enrolled me in a private girls' school in Paris. Since Gene was only four at the time, the same girls' school agreed to accept my little brother too (I often wonder what he must have thought about that). In no time, I was speaking French! When the war broke out, we managed to catch the last ship back to America. Since then, I've returned to both Rome and Paris many times throughout the years and still find these two beautiful cities to be intoxicating. To this day, I can still speak both languages fluently.

School days

Upon our return to the United States, I began attending Merrick Middle School. Almost immediately, I found myself being bullied by some of the kids regarding my Italian heritage, having just returned from there. It got to be so bad, that my mother actually took my brother and I down to the courthouse and legally had our names changed from Canizaro to Benedict (Benedict being my father's first name). It was a drastic step to be sure, but one which ultimately worked.

Soon, the bullying subsided and I began to really enjoy school. These were great times. We would have sleepovers and never had to lock our doors. Of course, it was a much safer world back then. In fact, I would walk to school by myself, taking a short cut through the woods. Following my graduation from Merrick, I was enrolled in Mepham High School. My high school days were fabulous and I never missed a dance. And of course there were lots of boys!

There was Richard who built model airplanes, Irgy who was quite the dancer and another boy whose piano playing was much more interesting than he was. And then there was Stan. Stan and his twin brother Jerry were the stars of the basketball team. Stan and I went steady and he let me wear his letterman's jacket. I was crazy about Stan!

I also had a friend named Mary Jane. I thought she had the perfect family. Her dad would always be home by 6 p.m., and, frankly, I was a bit jealous. Later, she confided in me that her father was one of the worst drunks in the world. After hearing some of her horror stories, I began to think that maybe my own family situation wasn't so bad after all.

Despite my traumatic oceanic experience at Jones Beach years earlier with my father, I found myself returning to it on a regular basis during my teenage years. Why? Well, because of all the boys! I remember a lifeguard there named Bob who was drop dead gorgeous. One night, he invited me to a party with all the other lifeguards. I was still only fifteen at the time. As soon as my mom found out about the party, she immediately came and "rescued" me away from the lifeguards.

During my senior year, I began babysitting a seven year old boy named

Merle Johnson who lived across the street. I think I got paid around fifty cents a night. The thing that I remember most was that his nose always seemed to

Basking in the sun at Jones Beach, Long Island, NY, not far from the lifeguard station

be running. Merle would later grow up to become Warner Brothers' contract actor and teen heartthrob Troy Donahue. Troy eventually married my good friend, actress Suzanne Pleshette.

Now, as an example of just how small a world Hollywood really is, consider this . . . My husband, actor John Myhers, and I attended Suzy and Troy's wedding in 1964. Prior to that, John had appeared along side Suzy and Tom Poston in the Broadway play *The Golden Fleecing*. I myself had worked with Tom on the original *Steve Allen Show*. Following Troy and Suzy's divorce, Suzy and Tom, who were now appearing together on *The Bob Newhart Show*

HENRY MILLER'S THEATRE

PREMIERE PERFORMANCE, OCTOBER 15, 1959

COURTNEY BURR and GILBERT MILLER

present

GOLDEN FLEECING

A New Comedy by
LORENZO SEMPLE, JR.

starring

TOM POSTON

with

CONSTANCE FORD	ROBERT ELSTON
RICHARD KENDRICK ROBERT CARRAWAY	JOHN MYHERS
MICKEY DEEMS	RALPH STANTLEY

and

SUZANNE PLESHETTE

Production Designed and Lighted by
FREDERICK FOX

Incidental Music by
DANA SUESSE

Directed by
ABE BURROWS

My future husband John Myhers co-starring with Tom Poston and Suzanne Pleshette in The Golden Fleecing

got married. See what I mean about Hollywood being a small world? But wait, I'm getting way ahead of myself...

While attending Mepham High, I was invited to dances at West Point by older boys who were in the military. I actually was too young to get on the base, so I fibbed about my age. The dances were very prim and proper and everything was planned out in advance. Upon entering the hall, the girls would be given cards telling them which dances they were required to dance, along with the names of the boys they would be dancing with! It was all a bit too stuffy for me.

West Point Hops dance assignments

Also during my senior year at Mepham High, an event occurred which would have a devastating impact on our family dynamic. One night my father, who had been drinking, showed up at our house with two showgirls! The rest of us were having dinner, and needless to say, a heated argument between my parents ensued. It ended with my father lifting up the dining room table and my mother yelling, "Kids, pack your things. We're moving to Florida!" At that moment, my parents made the decision to separate.

I never questioned my mother's wisdom, but I must say I was devastated to leave Mepham High, and especially Stan! I would now have to finish out my senior year at Miami High. As usual, I was able to adapt rather quickly.

A couple of months before the end of the school year, my father came down to Florida for a visit. Miraculously, my parents had decided to reconcile.

Enjoying a beautiful day at the Bahia Mar Yacht Center in Ft. Lauderdale, FL

I was ecstatic. During this visit, my mother told him I wanted to be an actress. My father loved the idea. A decision was made for him to return to New York right away while the rest of us stayed behind in Florida until after my graduation.

Soon, my father had rented us a new apartment on Park Avenue and had made arrangements for me to begin working with the very best drama teachers and talent agents the minute I arrived back in New York. I couldn't have been more excited. My parents were going to be together and I was going to finally get to fulfill my dream of being an actress. We were all set for a new beginning.

However, a week before I was to graduate from Miami High, my mother received a call from my aunt. Something had happened at the Chelsea Hotel where my father was staying. We had to immediately rush back to New York. I was forced to miss my graduation ceremony. The news coming from the hotel was incomprehensible.

In an instant, everything had changed . . .

Chapter 3

The Mystery of the Chelsea Hotel

IMMEDIATELY UPON OUR ARRIVAL in New York we returned to the house on 7th Street. It was a chaotic scene. My aunts and uncles were all trying to gather information on what exactly had transpired. The news trickling out of the Chelsea Hotel and from the police was surprisingly vague and disjointed. All of us wanted to know what really had happened at that hotel, but trying to pry the specifics from the investigators was next to impossible.

Ever since I was a little girl, I'd always had this uneasy feeling or premonition that my father would meet an untimely death. I figured it would probably be the result of a car accident or something similar. However, I never could have imagined that this would happen. Tragically, he was only forty years old at the time.

The Chelsea Hotel on 23rd St. in New York City, NY

From what little the police were telling us, this is what we knew: My father Ben had mysteriously fallen out of a fifth story window at the Chelsea Hotel at around 3 a.m. and had died instantly. Of course, I was in hysterics. How could this have happened? A superficial investigation into the incident quickly resulted in an official ruling of "accidental death." But something just wasn't adding up.

My father was a big sports fan. He would often go to boxing matches and other sporting events and place large bets on the games. On this particular afternoon, he had gone to the races and had won big . . . really big. He had $250,000 in cash on him when he entered the hotel earlier that evening with two other unknown men. Despite the fact that two of his diamond rings and all of the money was now missing, investigators insisted on classifying the death as an accident. They claimed that he simply fell out the window. But how? And why?

My father had often associated with shady characters in the past and it had finally caught up with him. The two men with my father that night were never publicly identified or brought in for questioning. Obviously, this was no accident. Anyone could clearly see it was a robbery/murder. But the investigators refused to look any further. An all-encompassing cover up was in full swing. For whatever reason, the falsified ruling of accidental death was allowed to stand.

Eventually, my mother received a large insurance pay out and the matter was quickly dropped. When I got older, I tried my best to get to the bottom of what had happened, but didn't have any luck. The mystery of my father's death would, unfortunately, forever remain a mystery.

A few days later we went to my father's funeral. I remember seeing the casket and being overcome with emotion. It was terrible, and I simply lost it. For years following the funeral, I would have awful nightmares of seeing my father buried alive. And then one night, I had a dream where he came to me, and in a comforting manner reassured, "I'm leading another life now." From that moment on, the nightmares stopped, never to return.

Years later, a writer friend of my husband John moved into the Chelsea Hotel and asked if I could come visit him. He was staying on the eighth floor and had heard that I was in New York. I was very hesitant to say the least. I had never been to the hotel, and because my father had died there, I had no intention of ever going there. A number of my celebrity friends had stayed at the hotel over the years, but there had never been a reason for me to stop by . . . until now.

I began praying that I would be able to get past the fifth floor without incident. It was a struggle getting on that elevator, but I made myself do it. I did manage to make it beyond the fifth floor and up to the eighth, and the writer and I wound up having a very nice time together. Of course, I did think of my father while I was there but chose to focus on my positive memories of him rather than his death. This ability, to be able to zero in on the positive aspects of those I loved, had become an essential trait I would tap into throughout the course of my life.

The question was... what were my mother, brother and I going to do now? The Park Avenue apartment that my father had rented for us would be too much of a financial strain on my mother without him. We had to reorganize. My mother chose to move us to Baldwin in Long Island instead. She soon got a job as a real estate broker and eventually became very successful.

Across the street from our new house lived the Meinch family. They had two sons. One of them was named George. At the time, I was sixteen and George was twenty-seven. We became friends and soon secretly began to date. George had been the captain of his football team. He was big and athletic and, as I would later learn, very artistic. He had received numerous athletic scholarships to various universities but suddenly, World War II had entered the picture and changed everything for him. He had been picked to be part of the landing at the beach in Normandy and, although he was lucky to have survived, his knee got shot up pretty badly.

With his athletic career in ruins, George was at a loss as to what he was going to do now. But he seemed like a nice guy and we got along well. Of course, I was still recovering from the death of my father. One day, out of the blue, George suddenly asked me to marry him! He gave me a rather expensive engagement ring and without really thinking about it, I accepted.

Needless to say, my mother was dead set against our engagement. For one thing, she thought I was way too young, and she of course was right. Once again, she decided to send me away—this time to Buenos Aires in Argentina! She even managed to fast track a new passport for me. However, on this occasion things would be different. I was going to stand up for myself and say,

"No, I'm not going!" There was just no way I was going to be shipped off to South America. George's parents tried to break off our engagement as well. But between him and me, we were far too stubborn to let anyone tear us apart.

My mother was not about to cancel her plans to send me away. So George and I made the life changing decision to elope. At the time, I was attending Hofstra College in Hempstead. One night at around 2 a.m., we packed up his car and began a cross-country adventure that would take us 3,000 miles away to the sunny shores of California . . .

Chapter 4

California Dreamin'

I WANTED TO GET AWAY FROM NEW YORK as far as I possibly could and California certainly fit the bill. George had given me a wonderful engagement ring and although I loved it, I suggested we sell it to pay for the trip. George agreed. So we got in his Ford Coupe and took off. My mother immediately alerted the police, but they never were able to find us.

We stopped at a number of courthouses along the way in various states and tried to get married. But they all told us the same thing—we would have to get my parent's consent since I was underage. Well, of course, my mother would never agree to that. But then we learned of one state bordering California where parental consent wouldn't be an issue . . .

We soon arrived in Reno, Nevada, found the courthouse, and walked out of there a married couple. Because this was Nevada after all, we (erroneously) thought we might be able to increase some of our funds via gambling. We learned of a so-called "friendly" poker game at a nearby casino and decided to sit in. However, in no time at all we had lost all of our money. The next day we discovered that the poker game had been rigged, but it was too late to do anything about it. The thieves were long gone. Some honeymoon this was turning out to be!

We arrived in California with zero dollars to our name. We ended up having to sleep in the car. We had one orange and one candy bar to split between us. And when that was gone, we had nothing. I must say that going hungry was the worst thing I've ever experienced in my life.

Soon, George was able to get a job and we moved into a small apartment on West 23rd Street in Los Angeles. I got a job at a bank and we began to settle in. It was then I discovered that George was a terrific artist. So I encouraged him to develop his skills and helped him to enroll at the local art school.

After a few months, George's parents came out for a visit. I don't think they were too impressed. We were struggling to make ends meet, but at least we had food on the table and a roof over our heads. We wound up staying in California for about a year. During this whole time, I never called my mother. George meanwhile was beginning to have some emotional issues. At the time, I didn't know just how serious they were and I thought it might be best for us to return to New York.

The minute we arrived back in Long Island, George began having a really difficult time, experiencing terrible nightmares on an almost daily basis. Back then, no one knew anything about Post Traumatic Stress Disorder, a disease that was tormenting thousands of returning veterans, especially those that had been wounded. George's life had been forever altered by the battle he fought defending our country on the beach at Normandy—his promising athletic career over before it even had a chance to start. To make matters worse, our parents were on our case to get a divorce.

George never received any help for his emotional trauma and he began to drink. He was a mess. He often would drink and drive and soon caused two separate accidents. In those days, there were no treatments available for such people and I was way too young and naive to understand what was going on. The situation at home had become impossible. I began to seriously consider that maybe we should get a divorce. The problem was I was now pregnant!

My one and only child, my beautiful daughter Claudia, was born in nearby Rockville Center. I told myself I was going to be the absolute best mother I could be. Shortly after the birth, my mother helped me file for legal separation. George was now drinking non-stop. The situation on the home front had disintegrated to point that we felt it was in the best interest of my daughter and I to leave before things got any worse.

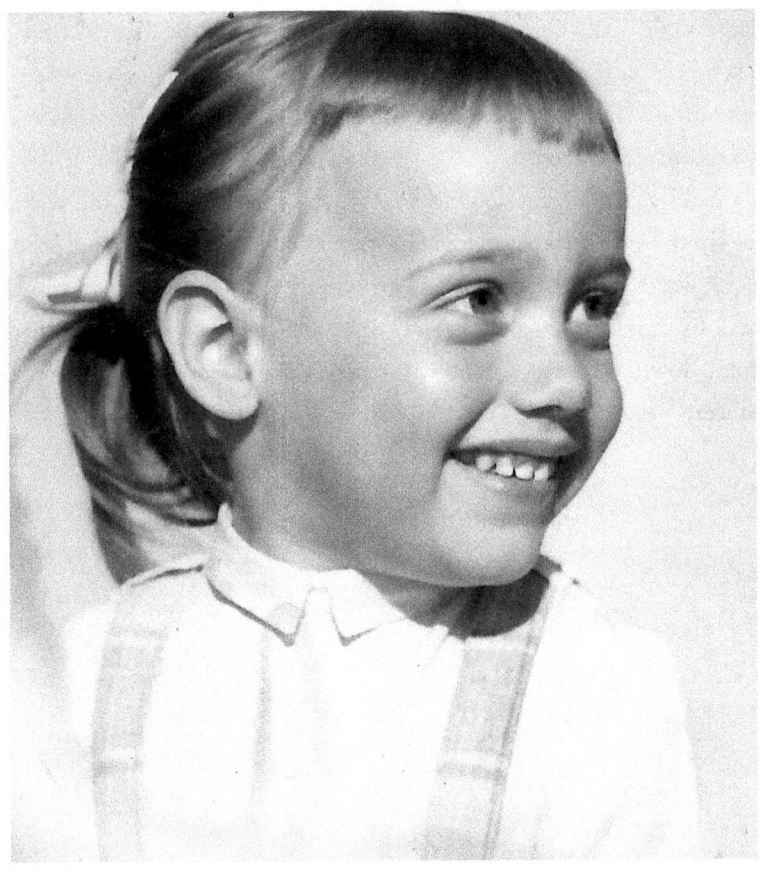

My daughter Claudia

The divorce became final around the time Claudia was about a year and a half old. Never once did I say anything bad to her about her father. But I was glad for my daughter and myself to finally be free of that situation. Years later, when Claudia was around fifteen, she began to correspond with her father. But by that stage, George was a good guy and no longer drinking. I had done my best to try and protect her, but suddenly, I was now the heavy. Unfortunately, the relationship between my daughter and I would become strained at that point.

Soon, I was able to attend my new drama classes and would commute to them via the Long Island Railroad. Meanwhile, my mother's real estate business was thriving. One day she sold a home to the head of Public Relations for TWA and was able to get me a job with them. Located in Rockefeller Center in Manhattan, TWA was looking for someone who could speak multiple languages. I started out as a receptionist and then moved up to becoming a secretary.

I had been there for about a year when a producer from the television game show *Strike It Rich* wandered in one afternoon. I told him I was studying to be an actress and asked if I could give him a call. He said, "Sure, why not?" I think I surprised him when I called up his office the next day. He asked me to come down to the studio, and within a week, I was working as an associate producer!

The journey I had been dreaming of since the age of seven was about to kick into high gear . . .

Chapter 5

This Could Be The Start of Something Big

During my year long stint at TWA, I continued to hone my acting skills under the guidance of a number of noted New York drama teachers. One of them, Miss Francis Robinson-Duff, was rather well known in the industry. However, she did have a few rather bizarre techniques that she would use, including having us lie on the floor and just breath. If my mother knew what was going on in these classes, I'm sure she would have thought they were a waste of time. Who knows, maybe they were. But this teacher sure had an impressive list of past clients including Clark Gable, Katharine Hepburn, Mary Pickford, and Helen Hayes.

I was also fortunate to be able to study with the legendary Betty Cashman at her studio located in Carnegie Hall. As soon as you climbed into the elevator, you could hear the other actors upstairs rehearsing through the elevator cage. A certain young Tony Curtis happened to be in my class. Her students however weren't limited to just actors, but included political figures such as NYC Mayor John Lindsay and CIA director William Casey, who were there to improve their public speaking skills.

This was the period when television quiz shows were all the rage. Joseph Cates was the producer of the infamous *$64,000 Question* along with a number of other programs. And I was now his associate producer. Joe would later go on to father actress Phoebe Cates *(Fast Times At Ridgemont High, Gremlins)* as well as produce and direct programs for Gene Kelly, Johnny Cash and Steve Martin. His younger brother, Gil Cates, also a well known producer/director, would eventually produce more Academy Awards telecasts than anyone else.

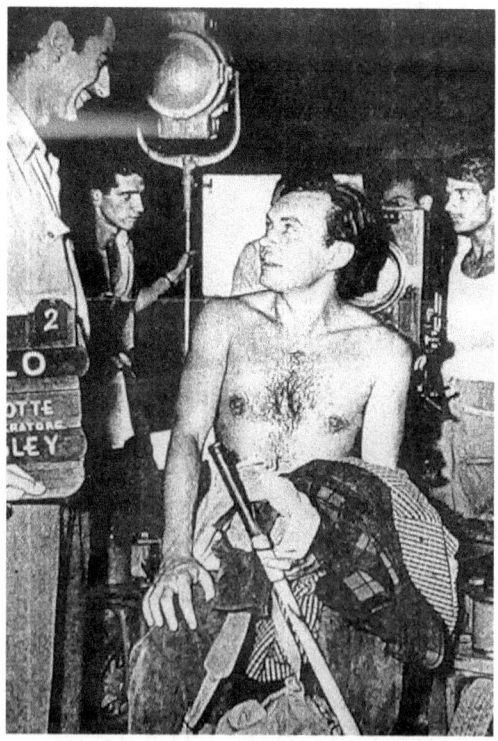

John Myhers at Cinecittà Studios in Rome

One day Joe announced, "Joan, we've got to get you going as an actress." I heartily agreed, of course. "We have an Italian version of *The $64,000 Question*," he added. "You speak Italian, right?" I let him know that I did indeed. So he introduced me to Tony Ford, an agent at William Morris who introduced me to the producer of the Italian version of his show, which was called *Win A Million Lire*. Tony explained, "We're sending the show's hostess back to Rome. We need a replacement right away; an actress who speaks Italian." I told him I was his girl.

The star of the show was John Myhers. Now here was a true renaissance man. He was a comedian, a dramatic actor, and he had the most wonderful singing voice. He had just returned from Italy himself. John had previously graduated from the MacPhail School of Music in Minneapolis and then, after the war, wound up staying in Rome following his discharge from the Army.

While there, John studied opera at the University of Rome along with cinema studies at Cinecittà Studios, home to the famous Italian directors Fellini and Rossellini. Upon graduation, he opened up his own nightclub there in Rome called The Jicky Club where he would showcase various entertainers and perform stand up comedy routines himself.

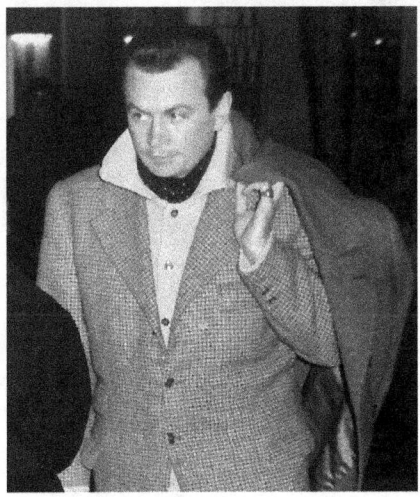

The dashing John Myhers in Italy

There was something special about John and we hit it off right away. It was my job to do the commercials . . . live, which is how they were done in those days. And they had to be in Italian. For each commercial, I made up all my own cue cards. They started me off by having me do the ads for Caffe Vivo on Saturday night as a test. Then after proving myself, they moved me over to the prime time show with John on Sunday nights. I was an immediate hit with the audience and became the hostess on *Win A Million Lire*.

One of my first TV jobs, when games shows ruled the airwaves

My appearance in ads and on various shows over the next few months attracted the attention of the highly respected William Morris Agency. A young agent there by the name of Bernie Brillstein, who had worked his way up in the company from the mail room, was assigned to represent me. Bernie would later go on to rep the likes of *Saturday Night Live* stars John Belushi,

Gilda Radner, Martin Short and Lorne Michaels along with *Muppets* creator Jim Henson. He would also produce blockbuster films such as *The Blues Brothers*, *Ghostbusters* and *Happy Gilmore*. But I was actually his first success.

Doing a promo for American Airlines

Bernie got me the gig as the National Hazel Bishop Cosmetics spokeswoman on *The Steve Allen Show*, and it was Bernie who got me my first chair with my name on it. That's when you know you've made it in Hollywood—having a chair on the set with your name on it. Appearing on the top rated *Steve Allen Show* was the big break I had been hoping for, and it would also be Bernie's first big achievement over at William Morris, as he would tell me years later.

There were loads of other girls auditioning for the part that day, but I nailed it. I became the show's commercial spokeswoman, just like I had done previously. It was a wonderful time. I did the commercials for about a year and then they asked me to join the cast of *The Steve Allen Show.* Suddenly, I found myself working alongside Steve and other series regulars like Don Knotts and Tom Poston. It was a hilarious comedy program where we would do these off-the-wall sketches live with cue cards.

The cast of The Steve Allen Show *(can you spot me, Tom Poston and Don Knotts?)*

Each morning I'd stop in to see how the writers were coming along. They nicknamed me "Boots" because I sometimes would wear red boots to the studio. We would always be joking around—it was all just so fabulous. Everyone connected to *The Steve Allen Show* was incredibly funny. Steve himself was just brilliant. Between takes he would play the piano. During the course of his life, he must have written over a thousand songs, which included his signature hit *This Could Be The Start Of Something Big.*

The show would frequently feature a different celebrity guest each week. One time, I was doing a skit where I was supposed to wear a gold swimsuit. A woman came up behind me and commented, "You sure do something for that bathing suit." I turned around to see Ginger Rogers herself standing there! At the time, I didn't tell her that it was her film *Top Hat* that had inspired me to get into the business, but maybe I should have.

Like John Myhers, Steve Allen was a renaissance man—a great musician, interviewer, comedian and all around entertainer. Steve and I stayed friends until his passing in 2000. He would often come to our house for dinner.

I know that one of the low points in his life occurred when some studio executive decided to get rid of all of the master tapes to his television programs which had been recorded throughout his extensive career. They were being stored in a film vault on the studio lot and apparently they needed the space. This short sighted executive figured that since the shows had already been broadcast, the masters would no longer be needed. Now this was before the advent of home video. These programs could have easily been transferred to DVD and marketed to the public. Decades of brilliant classic comedy sketches featuring some of the industry's biggest stars were now gone forever, unnecessarily. Steve was devastated by the news, along with millions of his fans.

Sometime later, John Myhers suggested I go over and meet with a friend of his who happened to be a producer on the highly popular show *Candid Camera*. I auditioned and got the job. *Candid Camera* was of course the original hidden camera show where unsuspecting people were filmed getting pranked. The first skit I did involved me wearing this ridiculous hat featuring a huge feather. I was supposed to ask some man for directions while making sure the feather ended up in his face.

He was a really nice man who was willing to help this apparent damsel in distress. I felt so guilty. But to be honest, he was the perfect victim. I wound up getting the feather in his nose, in his ear . . . and he just kept giving me directions. The undercover producer was there off to the side giving me signals, so I just kept the bit going for as long as I could. Arthur Godfrey

The classic Candid Camera *sketch featuring me wearing the infamous "feathered hat"*

was the host of *Candid Camera* at the time. After the segment aired, he said I should have gotten an Academy Award for my performance. Even today, that bit is considered one of the program's all-time classics.

After that, show creator Allen Funt wanted to sign me to the show full time. I did do a number of other segments including one where I didn't have enough money to pay for my cab fare. At first, they had me made up to look exceptionally beautiful. The cab driver was extremely nice and offered to come by my house later that night to collect the fare (or just come by the house to collect something else). The second time they had me made up to look like an old hag. This time, the cab driver was outraged that I couldn't pay and threatened to turn me in to the police!

This was all so very exciting. It was a wonderful time in my life. Other roles were coming my way on programs such as *Robert Montgomery Presents, The Art Ford Show* and *Kraft Theatre*. I was doing comedy, drama, theater, television, a little bit of everything, and working all the time. I was even hired as a voice actor on countless foreign language films where it would be my job to "re-voice" or re-dub the dialogue of famous actresses. For example, that's my voice you're hearing coming from the mouth of Bridget Bardot in the English language version of the motion picture *God Created Woman*.

I was starting to get recognized on the street and a number of men, both in and out of the business, began to ask me out. It was definitely the perfect time to be single …

As Helen of Troy in my first theatrical performance, Dr. Faustus…
The face that launched a thousand ships

Chapter 6

Indecent Proposals

I LOVE MEN. I love them because what you see is what you get. When I'm out and about, I notice that men, for the most part, just seem to be themselves. They talk, they interact with each other and they have a good time. Men are wonderful. Women on the other hand have to check each other out. "Look at her," they say. "I bet she's had some work done . . . on her face . . . definitely on her boobs. What is she wearing? That blouse does not go with those shoes! I can't believe she's showing that much cleavage! What a whore!" Yeah, men are more fun.

As mentioned, I had first met John Myhers while working on the Italian version of *The $64,000 Question* quiz show during the mid-1950s. John, in his larger than life style, had greeted me my first day on the job with a hearty,

"Welcome aboard." John was handsome, multi-talented, successful and very, very funny. The crew had warned me about John, describing him as a ladies' man. And as he was in the midst of a prolonged divorce, I knew that it might be best to look elsewhere—at least for the time being.

Back then, there was no shortage of datable young actors in New York to choose from. In fact, they seemed to be coming out of the woodwork. I was very much attracted to those who were in the arts—actors, musicians, artists, etc. I could easily relate to people, men especially, who were creative. I was young and still very naive. But I was also single and filled with the joy of life. Every relationship had the potential to be hotter and more passionate than the previous one. Yes, there was lots of sex to be had if one were so inclined.

The PR photo which lead to my doubling jobs for Elizabeth Taylor and Gina Lollobrigida

One young actor I dated during this period was Steve Cochran. Steve, who was smolderingly handsome and sexy with piercing blue eyes, had appeared in a number of big films during the late 1940s including *The Best Years of Our Lives*, *The Chase* and *White Heat* alongside James Cagney. And throughout the 1950s and 1960s he guest starred on nearly every top television show on the air, including *The Twilight Zone*, *The Untouchables* and *Route 66*.

The smoldering Steve Cochran

I had been doing *Theatre Macabre* in The Village when Steve came down to see me. These Grand Guignol plays were designed to shock audience members with their horrific images, but were in reality a lot of fun to do. I always seemed to get cast as a nurse assisting a murderous doctor in some sort of gruesome operation. After this particular performance, Steve asked me out. We went to the famous 21 Club on West 52nd. We had an amazing time and continued to see each other. He had a fabulous penthouse and was a smooth talker. I thought he was just wonderful, and the affair we had was simply incredible.

One day Steve invited me out on his yacht. What girl in their right mind would not want to spend the day aboard a beautiful yacht with a handsome and successful young actor? Yet, intuition told me not to go. I felt very strongly that something wasn't quite right, so I declined. It was this same kind of intuition I had felt leading up to the death of my father. It's hard to explain, but I've always had this sense about things. I still have it today and it has served me well, guiding me to make good choices throughout my life.

A few years later, Steve was found dead on that very yacht. Authorities discovered the boat carrying his lifeless body drifting off the coast of Guatemala. While the official cause of death was ruled acute lung infection, many believed foul play had been involved. It was my understanding from those who were in the know that he had indeed been murdered.

For a while, I dated noted television director Brooks Clift, older brother to actor Montgomery Clift. Monty had appeared in a number of films opposite Elizabeth Taylor and the two were dating at the time. Brooks kept asking if I wanted to go on a double date with his brother and Liz. This would be the first of a number of occasions throughout my life where Liz's name would come up and our paths would cross. Little did I know that I would be working alongside her very soon.

I have always been attracted to men's voices and I soon began dating several well known announcers. I refer to this part of my life as my "announcer period" where I actually dated four different announcers in a row. One was Bob Williams who lived on the Upper East Side. Another was the very funny

Elizabeth Taylor and me on the set of Butterfield 8

and articulate Lee Vines, announcer of the original television game show *What's My Line?* Then there was the 6-foot-4, blue-eyed Fred Maness, the voice of the old Universal newsreels. I remember he had a big white Continental that we would ride around town in.

Another gentleman whose voice I adored was actor/singer Johnnie Johnston. Previously married to well known actress Kathryn Grayson, Johnnie had been responsible for singing the haunting theme from the film *Laura*.

I admit, his singing voice "sent me" as I'm sure it did for a lot of girls around the country. We had met at a wrap party for a show I was working on. He was sitting at the piano and asked me to sit next to him. Our friendship became serious and at one point he asked me to marry him, to which I politely declined.

PR photo of me and Fernando Lamas

During this time, I was also appearing on the television game show *Masquerade Party*. It was a very popular show which featured a different

Dancing with a masked Rod Steiger on Masquerade Party

A very handsome Rod, back in the day

celebrity guest each week wearing a mask. Viewers would try and guess their identities as they appeared in a series of skits. Through the program I was able to meet and work opposite a number of big stars including Fernando Lamas and Rod Steiger. Rod and I hit it off immediately and began to date. Often Rod would take me to 21 where he had his own private table, a table that had previously belonged to Humphrey Bogart.

Nearly every celebrity who has ever dined in New York, along with every U.S. President since FDR, has eaten at 21 at one time or another. In the past, the club also served as the home to the private wine collections of such luminaries as Joan Crawford, Judy Garland, Gene Kelly, Marilyn Monroe, Aristotle Onassis, Frank Sinatra and Elizabeth Taylor. Today, whenever I'm in New York, I make it a point to go to 21 where they still seat me at Rod's old table.

This was all pretty heady stuff for a young woman who was relatively new to the business. Rod was an icon and I was certainly smitten by his charm and good looks. Things could have gone further with Rod at the time had we both allowed it. However, he was about to head back to Hollywood to do another film and I was working steadily in New York. So we said our goodbyes. But there was definitely a connection there. Once back in Malibu, Rod would call me from his beach house asking if I wanted to join him out in California. But it just wasn't to be ... at least, not yet ...

Around this time, a casting director suggested I meet with director Daniel Mann, who was getting ready to begin pre-production on what would be Elizabeth Taylor's final film for MGM titled *Butterfield 8*. Daniel asked me out. But for some reason, I declined. Daniel was the type of director who liked to do a lot of rehearsals. Unfortunate for Daniel but fortunate for me, Liz refused to do them. So they ended up hiring me to take her place during the rehearsals. I also wound up doubling for Liz once production began. The whole project lasted about a year and I had a wonderful time. As a thank you, the producers added a one line part for me in the film as a secretary. To this day, I still get residuals for that one line!

Joan Never Slips Standing-In for Liz

While shooting the opening scenes of "Butterfield 8," in New York, Elizabeth Taylor had to wander around a bedroom in her slip. So Joan Benedict, her Stand-In, had to wander around in her slip.

Only Joan did more wandering in her slip than Elizabeth did in hers. Stars always rest more than Stand-Ins.

The little old man, serving as receptionist, outside the set, guessed that Liz was important, but was highly suspicious of Joan just in her slip. And once, when Joan, came flying by, answering a call to stand in, the man clucked in exasperation and sympathy:

"**Haven't you got any clothes? I'm going to buy you a dress.**"

When the warm indoor slip scenes moved to the cold outdoor slip scenes, there was a wait for lighting changes one morning, and Liz sat down and slipped her mink around her. When she looked up, saw Joan shivering, Liz quickly pulled the mink off, handed it to her Stand-In, and said: "Here, Joan. Put this on. You're really cold." Joan was grateful.

"**You've got to be crazy or love this business,**" Joan said, "or maybe both. When we went up state to Haverstraw it was 15 degrees. And I was outside from 7 a.m. to 4:30 p.m. That's when a Stand-In really earns her pay."

Miss Taylor was in her warm trailer, except for her one scene, which took five minutes."

A STAND-IN has to resemble her star, and sit in for her when the lighting and camera shots are being set, so the star doesn't wear out or wilt. Joan is up at 5 a.m., on the set at 7, and works until 11 a.m. before the first scene for the star is ready. Then Joan continues until 7 p.m., and sometimes until one a.m. For this she gets $100 a day for ten weeks work. Silence can really pay.

"More important, you're seen," she said, "and I've been told that MGM wants to see me when the movie is finished. When they first called me for this I wasn't interested. But on the second call they wanted me to read for the part. So I went just to find out why they would want a Stand-In to read."

JOAN BENEDICT: SILENCE PAYS

The director, Daniel Mann, wanted to rehearse the scenes with an actress, so he could determine what he wanted and make the necessary cuts. And Miss Taylor does not like to rehearse.

"But she amazed me," Joan said. "I've seen her do quite a few scenes in one take. She knows what she's doing. For one scene in Greenwich Village, everytime they were ready to shoot her coming out of a car, a crowd would rush up, asking for an autograph or picture, and spoil the scene. She just waved goodbye to everyone, drove around the block, and when the crowd drifted away she raced back, and shot the scene before they could spoil it."

John Myhers with Viveca Lindfors in the film Weddings and Babies

By now, John Myhers was attempting to re-enter the picture. But his divorce still wasn't final, so I continued to date others. One incident that I will never forget involved actor Keenan Wynn. Keenan was a very prolific actor who appeared in well over a hundred major films and television programs. I had met Keenan on the set of the film *That Kind of Woman* starring Sophia Loren. I had a small part in the film and had taken some PR photos with the film's other co-star Tab Hunter.

One night Keenan and I were making out in a restaurant when John Myhers happened to walk in and see us. I had told John that I would be going out with Keenan that night and John somehow managed to track us down. I looked up and saw John standing there at the bar while Keenan continued to kiss me. Keenan was pretty drunk and was supposed to make an appearance on *The Tonight Show* that night. So we got up and grabbed the limo waiting outside for us. John followed us out.

The rain was coming down in buckets. As the car pulled away from the curb, I looked out the back window and saw John standing alone in the rain, getting drenched, with a heartbroken look on his face. It was just like in a scene out of a movie. As I watched John fade further into the distance, I could almost hear the sad music beginning to swell.

PR photo of Tab Hunter and me, from That Kind of Woman

The incomparable John Myhers

Chapter 7

The Hills Are Alive

JOHN MYHERS HAD BECOME a semi-regular guest on NBC's *The Tonight Show* during the late fifties and early sixties. Jack Parr had taken over the role of host on this pioneering and highly successful late night talk show from my old boss Steve Allen. Richard Rogers happened to be watching one night when John was on and was captivated by what he saw. Rogers, composer extraordinaire, was of course one half of the most successful writing partnership in American musical theater history. Together with lyricist Oscar Hammerstein, the two of them had created such classics as *Oklahoma, Carousel, South Pacific* and *The King and I,* and were about to embark on the their latest theatrical production called *The Sound of Music.*

John was in his usual classic hilarious form that night on *The Tonight Show*. Richard thought John would be perfect for the role of Max Detweiler, the lovable comedic caretaker of the singing Von Trapp family. They were holding auditions for the First National Touring Company of *The Sound of Music* and John asked me to accompany him to the theater. John was scheduled to audition alongside Florence Henderson (yes, the future Mrs. Brady!) who was a musical theater star at the time.

John and me with his Sound of Music *co-star Florence Henderson*

There were only five of us sitting in the audience of the Lunt-Fontanne Theatre watching the auditions that afternoon … myself, the director, producer Leland Hayward, Richard Rogers and famed actress and Broadway star (and future mother to Larry Hagman) Mary Martin. John's comedic timing was spot on, but then it came time for him to sing. And when he opened his mouth, things took a dramatic turn. Remember, John was no slouch when it came to singing. He had been trained as an opera singer and had spent time with the St. Paul Civic Opera.

> GARSON KANIN
>
> March 16, 1960
>
> My dear John,
>
> Here are my many thanks for your thoughtful letter which I greatly appreciated.
>
> You are a rare soul, dear John, and are one of the few good things to result from the production of THE GOOD SOUP.
>
> I live in hope that we may soon -- very soon -- renew our working relationship.
>
> Meanwhile, much love and my thanks for all you did and do.

He had recently appeared on Broadway alongside Ruth Gordon in the Garson Kanin adaptation of *The Good Soup*. And although John had been called in to audition for the role of Max, Richard immediately stopped the performance and loudly announced, "We found our Captain Von Trapp," which of course was the lead dramatic role.

John was signed then and there to a three year contract to perform *The Sound of Music* at all the major theaters in every major city around the country. The day before the tour was to begin, John and I had lunch with Richard Rogers at a cafe in New York. As we were talking, one of Richard's famous songs suddenly began to play over the restaurant's sound system and I felt my body start to tingle! Perhaps it was a sign at just how successful this tour was going to be . . .

> **Richard Rodgers**
> 488 MADISON AVENUE • NEW YORK 22, N. Y.
> Telephone MUrray Hill 8-2640
>
> June
> 2nd
> 1961
>
> Dear John,
>
> I love the picture of you and Florence and I rush to take my secretary in hand to tell you how grateful I am to have it. She is still prettier than you are, but you are manlier in every way.
>
> My reports from your tour are exhilarating and highly satisfactory. I would judge that you continue to be a wonderful company and all this makes me happy indeed.
>
> Thanks again and my love to all of you.
>
> Sincerely,
>
> Dick
>
> P.S. My secretary is studying typing.

And then John dropped a bombshell on me. He asked me to marry him and accompany him on tour! I had to think long and hard about that. His divorce was nearly final, but not quite. My career was going full force in New York. I had a fantastic apartment near Central Park on West 70th Street. Allen Funt wanted to sign me as a regular on *Candid Camera,* one of television's top rated shows. But John was just so fabulous, funny, talented and handsome. And he loved me with all his heart. I said "yes" and never looked back. I instantly knew it was the right decision.

Saying farewell to my New York apartment on W. 70th Street

The tour started off wonderfully with opening night in Detroit, and then moved to Chicago where the show would remain for a full year! *The Sound of Music* was a huge success and John's performances night after night were simply amazing. His divorce became final while we were in Chicago so we decided to wed right away. Chicago Mayor Richard Daley arranged for Illinois Superior Court Judge (and future President Kennedy-appointed Federal Judge) Abraham Lincoln Marovitz to marry us at the courthouse in between shows.

John and I tie the knot in Chicago

Famed *Chicago Sun-Times* columnist Irv Kupcinet and his wife Esther served as our Best Man and Maid of Honor. John and I spent the rest of the afternoon riding around town on a horse pulled carriage. From that moment on while we were in Chicago, John and I found our names in the gossip columns nearly everyday, thanks to Irv.

Once John and I were settled in, we sent for my daughter Claudia, who had been temporarily staying with my cousin Bob in California. Upon her arrival in Chicago, I told her how much I loved her and missed her. She immediately went up to her new stepfather John and asked him how long she could stay. His response was, "Forever." Claudia was excited to be with us on the road where she continued her school work alongside the other children who were part of the cast. I in turn continued my semi-regular work on *Candid Camera*, where they would fly me in from the tour whenever I was needed.

A most wonderful day for a wedding

John and me at the wedding reception with Irv and Esther Kupcinet

United States District Court
For the Northern District of Illinois
Chicago, Illinois 60604

Chambers of
Abraham Lincoln Marovitz
District Judge

February 9, 1965

Mr. and Mrs. John Myhers
8841 Evanview Drive
Hollywood 69, California

My dear Joan and John:

Christmas has come and gone but the memory lingers on. I am just getting around to acknowledging some of the little notes that came with the cards, one such as yours.

It was a delightful picture of both of you and you still look as much in love as you were the day I had the happy privilege of performing the marriage.

I am happy that you have kind thoughts of me and know that you will always be a very welcome visitor should you return to Chicago, either to visit or work.

With warm regards and the best of all good wishes -- think of me always as a good friend.

Sincerely,

Abe Marovitz

WESTERN UNION TELEGRAM
W. P. MARSHALL, PRESIDENT

LLP103 BA066
B RIA016 PD RI NEW YORK NY 13 1049A EDT

1962 JUL 13 AM

MR AND MRS JOHN MYHERS, THE SOUND OF MUSIC CO
SHUBERT THEATRE CHGO ILL
YOUR NEWS IS WONDERFUL AND I SEND YOU BOTH MY DEEPEST GOOD
WISHES FOR YOUR HAPPINESS LOVE
DICK RODGERS

THE WHITE HOUSE
WASHINGTON

July 15, 1963

Dear Mrs. Myhers:

The President has asked me to acknowledge your letter of July 8th, suggesting that he and his family see "The Sound of Music" which is currently playing at the National Theatre.

Although he appreciates your thoughtful suggestion, the President feels there is little likelihood they can do this. His family is away for the summer, and he does not know of a time when he could see "The Sound of Music."

The President is grateful for the kind comments you made in your letter and sends his thanks and best wishes to you.

Sincerely,

Kenneth O'Donnell
Special Assistant to the President

Mrs. Joan Benedict Myhers
International Inn
14th and M. Streets, N. W.
Washington 5, D. C.

Although President Kennedy was unable to attend the show, we were invited to meet him at a White House Press Conference

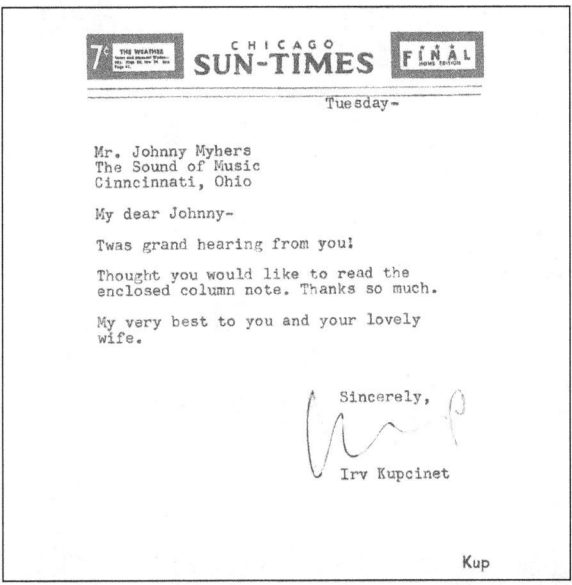

Shortly after the wedding, John and I were invited to the home of an extremely wealthy aristocratic family for dinner. With John being the outlandish person that he was, I should have known the evening might be a bit challenging. This family was so rich, they had their own vault where they stored all their gold—which they proceeded to give us a tour of! At dinner, the matriarch asked how John and I met, to which John replied with a straight face, "Well, she was running a whore house outside of Barstow, and I suppose it was love at first sight."

After a year, the touring company had completed its run in Chicago and would now be traveling for the next two years to other cities across the country. The production company chartered us our own private train to take us from city to city. And what a production it was! We had all the sets, more than fifty musicians, and a huge cast that included children, tutors, and their mothers all traveling with us. Frankly, it was insane.

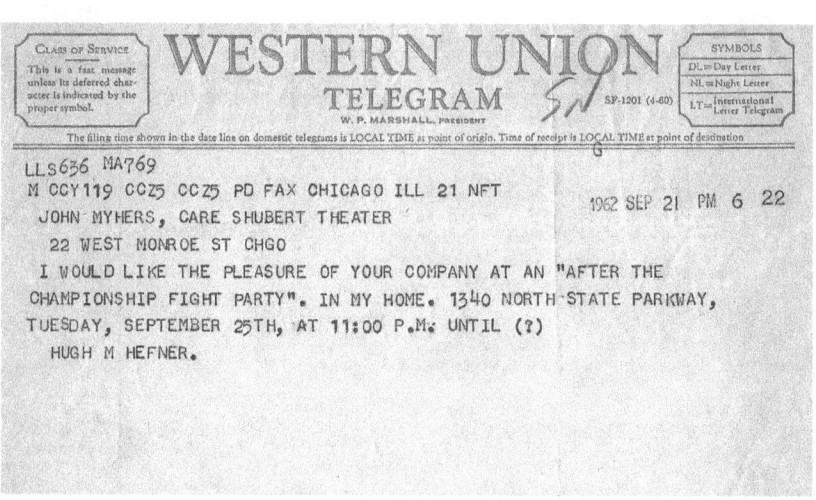

The success of The Sound of Music *got us invites to all sorts of places*

There was a John Myhers Day held in his hometown of Eau Claire, Wisconsin, complete with a parade!

John and Florence Henderson promoting The Sound of Music *on national TV*

Nearly all of the shows were sold out. The public couldn't get enough of John. And then there were those parties almost every night. I was commuting back and forth between whatever city we happened to be in and New York, appearing with John Cassavetes on his series *Johnny Staccato*, along with other acting gigs. The whole thing eventually took its toll. At one point, I came down with pneumonia and was bedridden for six weeks.

The star of the show in his dressing room

As the tour continued, everyone was getting rich. Many of the women who were part of the production began purchasing mink coats which were all the rage back then. At one point, there were so many new trunks having to be loaded and unloaded that Company Manager Herman Bernstein lost it one day and yelled at the actresses to quit buying stuff.

Actress Lainie Kazan was part of the chorus and was always after John. Sometimes I think John's co-star Florence Henderson may have been interested in him as well.

Looking back, some of the occurrences on that tour were rather amusing, while others were downright scary. One of the children who was a cast member tried to burn down the hotel we were staying at in Boston. Another

John in his Sound of Music *dressing room*

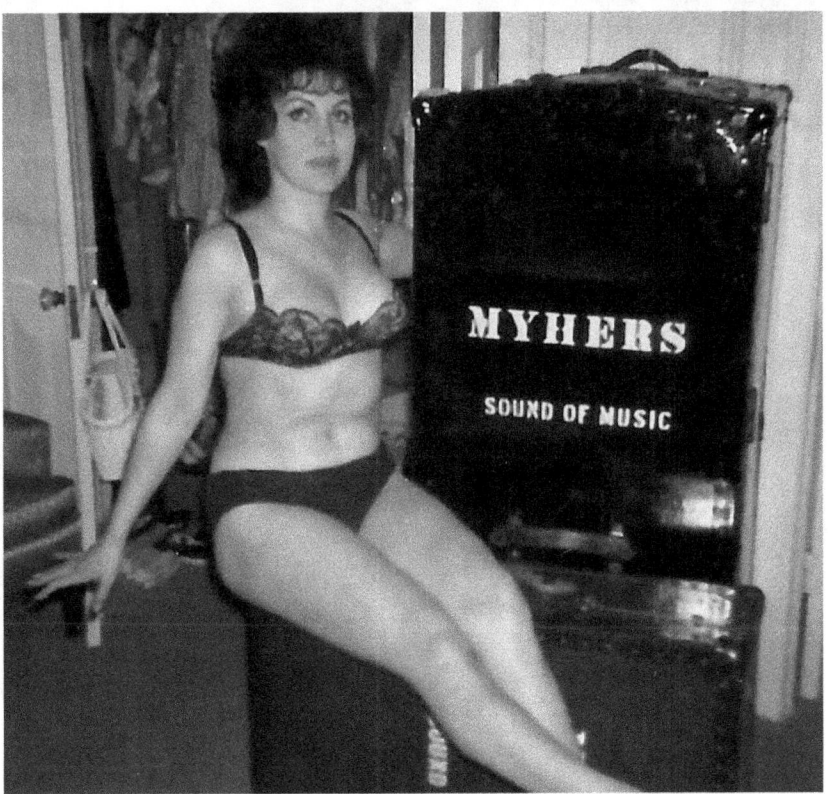

Me in John's Sound of Music *dressing room. Uh…*

John and I after one of his Sound of Music *performances*

John with the new Maria, Barbara Meister

LELAND HAYWARD · RICHARD HALLIDAY · RICHARD RODGERS · OSCAR HAMMERSTEIN 2nd
present

BARBARA MEISTER   JOHN MYHERS

IN THE AWARD WINNING MUSICAL

THE SOUND OF MUSIC

MUSIC AND LYRICS BY

RODGERS & HAMMERSTEIN

BOOK BY

LINDSAY & CROUSE

with

KATHERINE HILGENBERG   JACK COLLINS
and MARTHE ERROLLE

HELEN NOYES   REID KLEIN

Entire Production Directed by

VINCENT J. DONEHUE

Musical Numbers Staged by JOE LAYTON

Scenic Production by   Costumes by   Lighting by
OLIVER SMITH   LUCINDA BALLARD   JEAN ROSENTHAL

Orchestrations by   Musical Direction   Choral Arrangement by
ROBERT RUSSELL BENNETT   PETER LAURENCE   TRUDE RITTMAN

Original cast album by Columbia Records

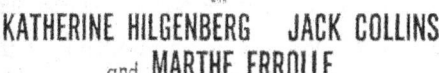

  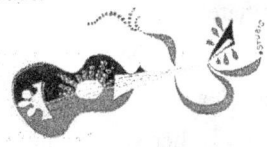

NATIONAL THEATRE
1321 E STREET N.W., WASHINGTON 4, D. C.
Limited Engagement Beg. Monday, June 17
FINAL PERFORMANCE SATURDAY NIGHT, AUGUST 24
Opening Night 8:00 -:- All Other Eves. 8:30 -:- Mats. Wed. 2:00 and Sat. 2:30
Prices: Mon. thru Thurs. Eves.—Orch. $6.95, $5.95; 1st Balc. $5.95, $4.95, $3.90; Upper Balc. $2.50
Fri. and Sat. Eves.—Orch. $7.90, $6.95; 1st Balc. $6.95, $5.90, $4.80; Upper Balc. $3.00
Wed. and Sat. Mats.—Orch. $5.50, $4.95; 1st Balc. $4.95, $3.95, $2.90; Upper Balc. $1.85
Please enclose self-addressed, stamped envelope for return of tickets

little girl peed on stage one night during a performance. And then there was the woman playing one of the nuns who was having an affair. Her husband found out about it and wound up murdering the man she was having the affair with!

Frequently, the train would stop in a certain city and the cast and crew would get off and go into town for supplies or to sightsee. But then the train would start to leave before everyone was accounted for and I would frequently watch as panic-stricken cast members raced to try and catch up to the train. One time, we started to pull away from a stop and I couldn't find John. I looked out the window in time to see him with suitcase in hand furiously running toward the train.

During the tour, we were invited to a Christmas party given by Mickey Rooney in honor of Judy Garland. I was so excited to finally get to meet Judy. It was during one of her low periods and she appeared to me to be a bit thin. Nevertheless, Mickey Rooney himself pulled the two of us aside and introduced her to me! Can you imagine that? Being introduced to Judy Garland by Mickey Rooney! There have only been a few times in my life that I have been overwhelmed meeting a Hollywood celebrity and this was one of them. I managed to maintain my composure long enough for us to exchange some small talk. I then excused myself, headed for the bathroom, locked the door and proceeded to break down and cry for about ten minutes. Fortunately, no one was the wiser.

Famed Hollywood columnist Hedda Hopper was also at the party that night. Her observations appeared the next day in newspapers all across the country. In her article, she made a point to say that she hoped John would reprise his role as Captain Von Trapp in the upcoming film version of *The Sound of Music* being planned by Fox, which was to begin production the following year. I think everyone who was part of the First National Touring Company felt the same way.

John and I safely on the Sound of Music *train*

> **Richard Rodgers**
> 488 MADISON AVENUE • NEW YORK 22, N. Y.
> Telephone MUrray Hill 8-3640
>
> October
> 15th
> 1962
>
> Dear Johnny,
>
> I was delighted with your letter and the clipping from the St. Paul paper. It seems hardly possible that we were all working together putting this company on its feet so long ago and it's a fine tribute to you that you're still at it.
>
> I did part of a symphony concert with Florence Henderson a week ago Saturday night and she and Ira spent Sunday with us in the country. I had wonderful news of you from her, full of enthusiasm and kind thoughts. Do have a good time and please keep the Captain in full charge of his company for us. All fondest regards.
>
> Yours sincerely,
>
> Richard Rodgers
>
> Mr. John Myhers
> "The Sound of Music" Company
> Shubert Theatre
> Chicago, Illinois

Richard Rogers always believed John had been the perfect choice to portray Captain Georg Von Trapp during the tour's extraordinary presentation of *The Sound of Music*. Throughout its phenomenal three year run, John had taken the part and made it his own. Nevertheless, when it came time to cast the movie version, John lost out to actor Christopher Plummer. Both John and I were beyond disappointed. Julie Andrews had already been cast. But apparently, Christopher Plummer managed to snag the role, in part due to existing contractual obligations he had with the studio. He also had the film's director, Robert Wise, in his corner.

John loved the character, and that love would have come through on the screen had he been given a chance to prove it. Plummer, on the other hand, couldn't hide his disdain for the role, a disdain which I couldn't understand. He often referred to the production as *The Sound of Mucus*. His less than stellar voice had to be re-dubbed by veteran studio playback singer Bill Lee in the final version of the film. Lee had previously been called upon to replace the singing voice of actors in other musical films of note including *Seven Brides for Seven Brothers*, *South Pacific* and *Mary Poppins*. Even though I probably witnessed more than 2,000 live performances of *The Sound of Music* during the course of our tour, to this day I've never taken the time to view the film, nor do I care to.

John and I in Hawaii during the run of The Sound of Music

In later years, John's association with the stage version of *The Sound of Music* would continue, but this time in an expanded role with himself as director. He led a highly successful run of the show in Las Vegas and another in Hawaii featuring Jane Powell. Even my daughter Claudia eventually got in on the act, effectively taking on the role of Brigitta Von Trapp.

With the exhaustive three year tour having now come to an end, and without John missing a single performance, it was time for the two of us to re-evaluate our options. Should we head back to the comfort and familiarity of New York? Or do we take our chances out west ...

John with The Sound of Music *co-star Jane Powell*

John with Claudia and me

Chapter 8

The Wild Wild West

DESPITE THE FACT THAT my previous venture out west had been a disaster (broke, hungry and living in a car), I was nevertheless excited to begin a new life with John in Hollywood where we could be near the studios. John's manager, Bullets Durgom of the famed management team Durgom & Katz, was selling his house on Evanview Drive in Sunset Plaza. So we bought it from him and moved in. Our neighbors included Sammy Davis Jr. on one side, and Jerry Schilling, a member of the Memphis Mafia, on the other. Elvis Presley himself had actually bought that house specifically for Jerry.

Me with our former neighbors Jerry Schilling and his wife

Ours was a beautiful home that had a gorgeous view overlooking the entire city, perfect for entertaining. The parties we threw at Sunset Plaza were the stuff of legends. John's and my birthdays were six months apart, which gave us an excuse to host these amazing gatherings at least twice a year and invite all our friends. I'll have more to reveal on this subject later, but suffice it to say that those who attended never left disappointed. Ultimately, John and I would spend nearly three decades accumulating priceless memories at the Evanview home.

Me outside our Evanview home

The move to Hollywood provided a catalyst which kicked both of our careers into high gear. From the moment we arrived, neither one of us stopped working. In a business where you're never quite sure when *or if* there will be another job, both of us felt confident that the opportunities would just keep coming . . . and they did!

One of our first projects together after the move was an ambitious motion picture conceived by John titled *Saturday Night Bath In Apple Valley*. It was a film destined to become one of the most unconventional and off-the-wall comedies of all time. John wrote, produced, directed and co-starred in this outlandish feature that was shot entirely in Apple Valley. The script had almost no narrative, just a lot of crazy things going on. Frankly, it was way ahead of its time.

Red Granger and me in a scene from Saturday Night Bath In Apple Valley

Me as Poopsie Patata taking a bath on a Saturday night in Apple Valley (hence the film's title)

On the way out to Apple Valley to scout locations, John and I brought our friend Walon Green with us. He was suffering from a hangover and complained the whole way up about having the top down on the car. Walon would go on to write films such as *The Wild Bunch* and even win an Academy Award. Eventually he turned to television, becoming one of its most successful writer/producers on programs such as *Hill Street Blues, ER, NYPD Blue,* and *Law and Order.* I like to think we gave him his start with *Saturday Night Bath.*

The threadbare plot concerned an unscrupulous gambler known as The Big Man (played by Phil Ford) who arrives one day in Apple Valley and tries to turn it into a gambling Mecca. Comedian Cliff Arquette, best known as a regular on *The Hollywood Squares* and grandfather to actors Rosanna, Patricia and David Arquette, appeared in his Charlie Weaver character as the mayor, but also showed up in drag as an old woman! I played The Big Man's girlfriend, Poopsie Patata, and we certainly had more than our fair share of laughs making the film.

John and I on the set of Saturday Night Bath in Apple Valley

John directs Red Granger in a scene from Saturday Night Bath in Apple Valley

Red Granger as The Cowboy and me as Poopsie Patata on the set of
Saturday Night Bath In Apple Valley

Me as Poopsie tickling the ivories

Red Granger, Mimi Rogers, Cliff Arquette and me on the set of Saturday Night Bath

It was supposed to be a modern day western, except that we had Vikings, Nazis and bullfighters all running amok. John portrayed a director trying to shoot a Tarzan movie in the middle of the desert with a ninety year old Tarzan. Meanwhile, the town council spent much of its time trying to figure out how to work an Ouija board. Poopsie was required to travel by stagecoach wherever she went, while The Big Man would have dreams of his mom washing him outdoors in a bathtub filled with money. Yes, my husband John was crazy, or brilliant, or perhaps both!

Cliff Arquette was pretty much drunk the whole time we were on location, which didn't seem to negatively affect his performance, and may have even enhanced it a bit. I do remember that a young man delivered a telegram to the set one day and was subsequently given a part in the film. John was able to cut a deal with Newton T. Bass, the founder/owner of Apple Valley, to let us use his town as well as his incredible mountain top mansion,

Cast member Mimi Hines and me, in matching outfits, practice our dance moves backstage, as a bewildered Claudia looks on

complete with an indoor swimming pool, for filming . . . all for free! In fact, John managed to get nearly everything deferred, meaning that it didn't cost a whole lot to make the film.

With John in charge of nearly all of the production work on the film, and me starring in it, we suddenly found ourselves with the nicknames of Desi and Lucy, bestowed upon us by our peers. Once the film was completed, we had a huge screening in Hollywood. Everybody we knew showed up and had a great time. Mickey Rooney was there, and I remember him making comments throughout the film, saying things like, "This is completely insane!"

John and me in front of Newton T. Bass' Apple Valley mansion

The Saturday Night Bath *cast gets wild at the wrap party*

The Saturday Night Bath *cast at the film's Chicago Film Festival premier*

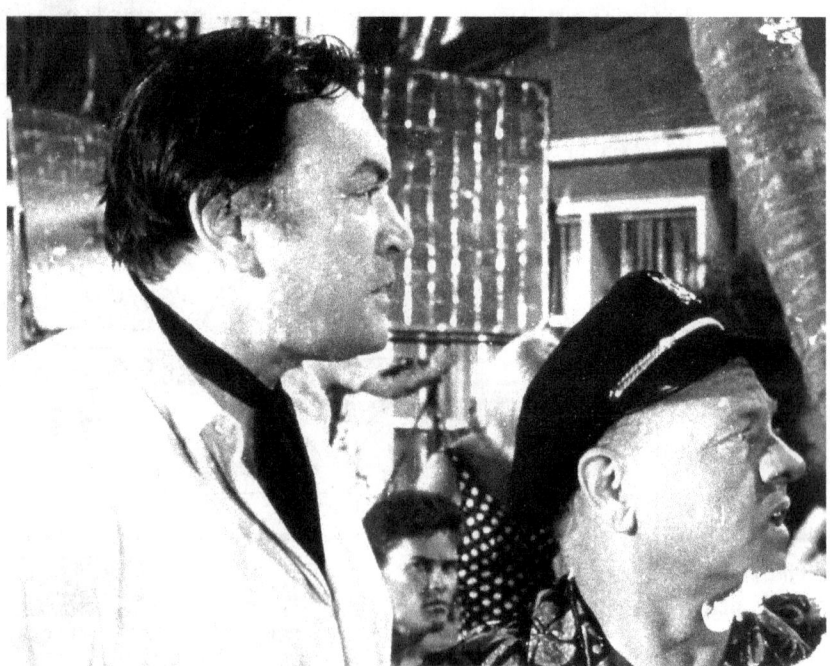
Mickey and John on the set of Mickey's sitcom

John and I had been good friends with Mickey Rooney for awhile before John was asked to appear on an episode of Mickey's sitcom, simply titled *Mickey*. By this time, Mickey was up to wife number five, Barbara Thomason, a blonde beauty who was seventeen years his junior. The four of us used to double date quite often. Mickey would drive all of us around in his big Lincoln and we just had so much fun. In 1965, when Mickey was away filming *Ambush Bay* with Hugh O'Brian in the Philippines, Barbara allowed a young actor from Yugoslavia named Milos Milosevic to come stay at their Brentwood home, and the two of them began having an affair.

After the film had wrapped, Mickey returned home to find his wife involved with this other man. Wanting to stay with Mickey, Barbara tried to break off the relationship with Milos, but there was a problem . . . Milos was known to have an explosive temper. He was not expected to take the news of being dumped quietly, so Barbara brought a couple of friends with her to the house for protection. To everyone's surprise, Milos seemed rather calm about the whole thing, so he and Barbara retreated to the master bedroom where they could talk some more. Suddenly, Milos grabbed Mickey's .38 pistol which he kept in the bedroom for protection and fired a single shot into Barbara, and then another into himself. Both of them died instantly.

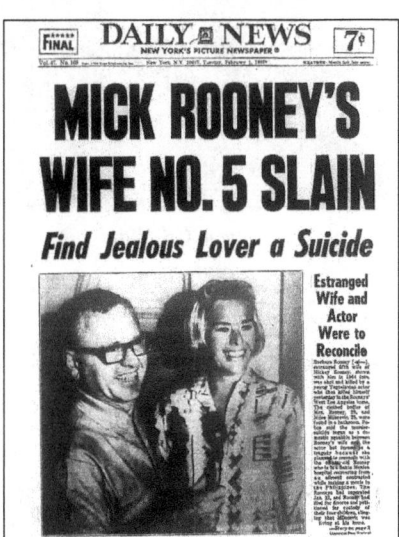

Years later, John had called Mickey on the occasion of his 50th birthday. Mickey was depressed that no one from MGM, the studio he had made millions for, had bothered to call him to wish him a happy birthday. After hanging up, John immediately got on the phone to MGM and had one of the studio heads give Mickey a call. Later that evening, Mickey called John back, excited that someone from MGM had cared enough to call. Mickey never found out that it was John who had arranged the phone call. John was just that kind of person.

Bob Crane as Col. Hogan

One of John's semi-regular roles was on the hit comedy series *Hogan's Heroes*. Each time he appeared, he was absolutely hilarious and the producers kept asking him back. I don't think he ever played the same character twice though. One week he would be Field Marshal von Heinke, the next General Wittkamper, and the next Colonel Schneider. I would go with him to the set and would come home exhausted from laughing so much.

John of course would always have to make a dramatic entrance upon his arrival to the soundstage in Culver City where the show was being filmed. Werner Klemperer, the actor who portrayed Colonel Wilhelm Klink, was the son of renowned orchestral conductor Otto Klemperer. So, as a tribute, John would march onto the set each day singing Klemperer's name over and over to the tune of some well known John Philip Sousa composition.

John with Hogan's Heroes *co-star Robert Clary*

WELCOME TO Stalag 13

THE BEST POW CAMP IN WORLD WAR II

Stay for a day and you'll want to
remain for the duration.

December 30, 1966

Mr. and Mrs. John Myhers
Empire Pictures, Inc.
8841 Evanview Drive
Hollywood, California

Dear John and Joan:

I am glad that you got the telegram and I hope that business is going well with you.

Your episode of Hogan's will be aired Friday, January 6, and according to all who have seen it think that it is the best Hogan's we have done in two years - many thanks to you.

Miss you - <u>both</u>.

Love and kisses,

Bob Crane

BC/j

The show's star, Bob Crane, had his drums set up in an area near his dressing room and would often play them during breaks between takes. Most people were unaware that Bob actually played the drums on the show's famous opening theme song. A few who worked on the show knew he was into some sexually creepy stuff, and although he seemed like a nice guy, I always had this feeling he would meet an untimely demise, just as I had felt with my father. And once again, I was right. To this day, Bob Crane's brutal murder in an Arizona apartment remains officially unsolved.

Chapter 9

The King and Queen of Sunset Plaza

JOHN HAD ALREADY BEEN DOING the voice of cartoon character Hector Heathcoat before we arrived in Hollywood. That work continued once we were in California, as did his guest appearances on a number of comedy shows, including multiple episodes of *Get Smart* where he was always so funny.

Due to the great reviews he had received from *The Sound of Music* run, John was able to land a role in the film version of the musical *How To Succeed In Business Without Really Trying* with Robert Morse and Rudy Vallee.

This was immediately followed by the comedy *The Private Navy of Sgt. O'Farrell* which we shot in Puerto Rico. The film starred Bob Hope, Phyllis Diller and Jeffrey Hunter. John was given Jonathan Winters's part, who had to back out of the project at the last minute. John of course did an amazing job. I doubled for Gina Lollobrigida in the film and did all of her bathing suit scenes on screen. John kept Bob in stitches the whole time we were on location. At the film's premier at Grauman's Chinese Theatre in Hollywood, Bob Hope introduced John as "the man who kept me laughing on and off the set."

John with Don Adams in a classic episode of Get Smart

During the shoot, Phyllis would host dinner parties for us every night. She of course was continually tipsy while we were there and constantly added booze to whatever she was cooking. I celebrated a birthday during the filming of *Private Navy* and the crew threw me this incredible party right there in San Juan. I'll always remember being kissed by Bob Hope on my birthday.

Next, John and I both appeared on the John Forsythe series *To Rome With Love*. I was then cast opposite Henry Fonda on an episode of his series *The Smith Family*. Henry Fonda was very nice as expected, but spent most of his time off camera trying to be funny. Candidly speaking, comedy wasn't his

John with Robert Morse in a scene from How To Succeed In Business Without Really Trying

John with Bob Hope on the set of The Private Navy of Sgt. O'Farrell

forte. But then again, I was used to the best. Not too many people can hold a candle to John Myhers.

Soon thereafter, John took on a change-of-pace dramatic role with *Willard,* a thriller about a young man who uses hundreds of trained rats to get revenge on his enemies. The film was directed by Daniel Mann, who had directed *Butterfield 8* a few years earlier. Bruce Davison, the actor who played the lead, became the boyfriend of my daughter Claudia. For awhile, they were talking marriage, but Claudia broke it off due to Bruce's abuse of alcohol at the time. Claudia then turned her attentions toward pop star David Cassidy. Bruce admitted to having a problem, but later on was able to get sober and create a wonderful career for himself.

My lovely daughter Claudia and me

During this time, John also did a whole slew of guest appearances on a number of well known sitcoms including *The Flying Nun, I Dream of Jeanie, The Doris Day Show, The Odd Couple* and *Alice,* along with a few guest starring roles on dramatic programs like *It Takes a Thief, The Waltons* and *The Bionic Woman.*

John as Admiral Brenner in Disney's The Shaggy D.A.

He also appeared on *Love, American Style* seven times in seven different roles, and in seven films for Disney including *Herbie Rides Again* and *The Shaggy DA*. John was also magnificent in the play *Idiot's Delight* opposite Jack Lemmon, which was directed by Garson Kanin at the beautiful Ahmanson Theatre in downtown Los Angeles.

While John was busy with all of that, I was concentrating on soaps. Now, this is where I turned in some of my best work, if I do say so myself. I started out on the long running daytime drama *General Hospital* doing what is known in the business as "under five," which meant that my character was given less than five lines of dialogue per episode. Union rules dictated that if an actor had more than five lines, his rate of pay would increase significantly. So to save money, the writers would be instructed by producers to keep the "under five" actors' dialogue at that level or below.

Now, there was a way to get around the union rules, and this was how it was done . . . they would purposely eliminate most of the periods in the script's dialogue. It was as simple as that! So, the scripts that I would get

Director Garson Kanin

would often be filled with these huge run-on sentences. There would be a significant amount of dialogue to learn, but technically, it would still be less than five lines. Eventually, the unions caught wind of their schemes and the rules were reworked so that sentences could no longer exceed fifty words, which if you think about it, is still a pretty long sentence.

Soon after meeting with the show's casting agent, I got moved up to one of the leading roles on *General Hospital*, portraying Edith Fairchild. Most of my scenes were opposite heartthrobs Tony Geary or Tristan Rogers. I wound up doing the show for three years and had a great time.

I also appeared on a few other soaps including *Days of Our Lives, Santa Barbara* and *Capitol* where they had me playing a nun! The time I had previously spent with The Actors Co-op and Actors' Alley prepared me for the sometimes difficult work and grueling hours. Studying under the famous acting teachers Bobby Lewis and Stella Adler was also tremendously helpful. Bobby would always say I was his favorite student and would come over to our house quite often to visit.

Me as a nun (obviously cast against type) on the soap Capitol

Me at Actor's Alley circa 1990

I loved doing soaps. But they were hard, mainly because of the amount of dialogue that had to be learned. It's not easy for me to remember lines anyway, but the writers would make it even more challenging by constantly doing rewrites at the last minute. And everything had to be done fast. Working on soaps was a great experience. Most people don't realize that a lot of stars like Brad Pitt, Susan Sarandon, Meg Ryan, Kevin Bacon, Demi Moore and Marisa Tomei got their start on soaps.

John continued to alternate between television and films, appearing in the motion picture *1776* over at Columbia and the independently produced mega-hit *Walking Tall* which was shot in Tennessee. This was followed by a campy R-rated feature called *Linda Lovelace for President*, a mainstream attempt to cash in on the massive popularity of *Deep Throat*. The all star cast included comedian Marty Ingels, who told John on the set that he himself was going to marry someone who looked just like me. And a year later, he married Shirley Jones!

THE Hollywood REPORTER

Joan Benedict Signed For 'Audrey Rose' Role

Joan Benedict has been signed for a role in "Audrey Rose," a Robert Wise Production for United Artists.

Starring are Marsha Mason, Anthony Hopkins, John Beck and Susan Swift in the title role.

The following year, both John and I appeared in a similarly themed film called *The Happy Hooker Goes to Washington* starring Joey Heatherton. John played a Washington Senator while I played Sally, Xaviera Hollander's boss. I actually had a really good part in an otherwise rather goofy film. George Hamilton also starred, appearing in the role of Ms. Hollander's lawyer. He was terrific and very sweet. The beautiful Joey Heatherton on the other hand was struggling with drugs during the film's production and sadly wouldn't accept anyone's help.

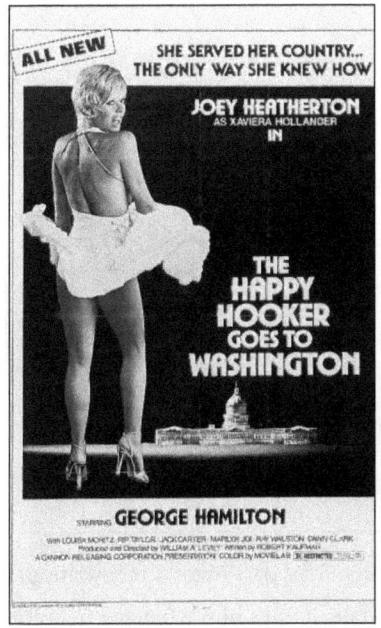 

The Happy Hooker Goes to Washington   *Filming the deleted courtroom scene for* Audrey Rose

I was then hired by noted director Robert Wise (*West Side Story, The Sand Pebbles*) to appear in his next film *Audrey Rose*, a supernatural thriller starring Anthony Hopkins and Marsha Mason. It was a big part and I spent weeks filming an elaborate courtroom scene, only to have the entire sequence edited out of the final version of the film by the studio. There were a group of real Hare Krishnas used in the courtroom scene and the studio did not want to risk causing any controversy by having Hare Krishnas appear in the movie. So out went my big scene. Welcome to Hollywood!

John and I both continued to work in television. We each did an episode of *The Incredible Hulk* and each did half a dozen *Fantasy Islands*, but we never appeared together in the same episode. And while John was doing *History of the World Part One* for Mel Brooks, I was busy guesting on shows like *Kojak* with Telly Savalas, *TJ Hooker* with William Shatner, and *Hotel* with James Brolin.

January 3, 1978

Ms. Joan Benedict
8841 Evan View Drive
Los Angeles, Ca. 90069

Dear Joan:

We are pleased to advise you that the segment of KOJAK entitled "JUSTICE FOR ALL" will be telecast on CBS, Saturday, January 7th at 10:00 p.m.

Sincerely,

Kathleen Rainey
Kathleen Rainey
Producer's Office

During this time, John continued to pursue his passion of screenwriting. I had gotten him a typewriter and he would take it with him wherever he went. I too was typing scripts for John almost all the time. It seemed that whenever my friend Suzy Pleshette would call up, I would be in the middle of typing a script. So she began to tease me about it and it quickly became an in-joke between us. According to her, "typing a script" was code for "having sex." For years she would say things like, "Well, Tom and I are going out for a romantic dinner, then afterwards we're going to come home and type a script."

Later on, John began to teach screenwriting. One of his young students was Paul Thomas Anderson, who would go on to write and direct numerous critically acclaimed films like *Boogie Nights* and *There Will Be Blood*. Paul's mom didn't think much of her son's movie business aspirations and it took John to convince her that Paul was indeed a genius. One night, after being nominated for his sixth Academy Award, Paul ran into my daughter Claudia, who asked him why he hadn't given John any credit for teaching him the ropes.

At my daughter Claudia's wedding, MountainGate Country Club, Bel Air, CA

Tim Conway and Don Knotts were two of our good friends and they were paired together in a number of comedy films during the 1970s and 1980s. Two of those films, *The Prizefighter* and *The Private Eyes*, were co-written by John and Tim. I appear in *The Prizefighter* playing Dori, the nightclub hostess. Set during the Depression, the film was shot in Atlanta and I do recall a lot of drinking going on. John also had a role in the film, and once again, we had a blast working on it together. And lucky for all involved, the film did quite well.

A year later, the boys were back at it with *The Private Eyes*, a spoof of classic Sherlock Holmes films. I believe *Private Eyes* to be one of John's best writing efforts. As a piece of trivia, I actually wrote one of the jokes that appears in the film. Tim and Don, dressed in their investigative attire, are knocking on the door of this house. A woman opens it and asks, "Are you from the Yard?" Don answers, "No, we're in the yard." The film was a massive hit, and eventually became the most successful motion picture to come out of Roger Corman's New World Pictures. A sequel was planned, but never realized. *The Private Eyes* was Tim and Don's best and, unfortunately, last collaboration on screen as a comedy duo.

Me with Don Knotts and Tim Conway in The Prizefighter

More scenes from The Prizefighter

Don Knotts and me in The Mind With The Dirty Man

During the mid-1980s, Don Knotts asked me to co-star with him in the play *The Mind with a Dirty Man* which we toured in Atlanta before coming to the beautiful La Mirada Theatre in California. We had a very successful run and the two of us really enjoyed working together again. But I have to admit, I never really considered any of it work. Being around these kinds of professionals was such a joy. During the period John and I were living in Sunset Plaza, Tim and Don were among the regular attendees at the biannual parties that we would have at our home.

Talk about fun . . .

Chapter 10

Party Central

COULD YOU IMAGINE throwing a party at your house with the likes of Jack Lemmon, Steve Allen, Tim Conway and Jonathan Winters providing the entertainment... for free? Most of our friends were celebrities and all of them were articulate, talented and simply brilliant. And when they came together at our house for one of our parties, there was magic in the air. Remember, these were some of Hollywood's best writers and comedians, so the laughter was nonstop. There were never any drugs around, but plenty of alcohol.

Don Knotts, Tom Poston, Bobby Morse and Buddy Atkinson, writer/producer of *The Beverly Hillbillies*, were just a few of the regulars. You couldn't wait for these parties to start because they were so much fun. Bea Arthur was usually already tipsy by the time she arrived ... and also barefoot for some reason. Lloyd Bridges was another attendee whom John had befriended while in Rome. One time Lloyd even brought his sons Beau and Jeff to the house.

My 50th birthday party at our Evanview home

Lloyd Bridges

Los Angeles 00, California

June 12th

Dear John,

Forgive the long delay in answering your letter, but my new series has been taking up absolutely every minute it seems.

Therefore, I haven't been able to even glance at the book you were kind enough to send me. In any event, I won't be free to do any important outside project for at least another year.

I'll be working straight through the summer, but if I ever have any free time I'll try to read the biography and give you my reaction.

Glad you are enjoying your work so much and meeting with such success.

Dotty joins me in sending fond regards to you and Joan.

Fondly—

Bud

The team of Jonathan Winters and John Myhers would of course have everyone rolling on the floor within minutes. And at times, John would spontaneously burst into song. On one occasion, Andy Griffith got annoyed with his wife and complained, "Why is it that every time John sings, you feel the need to compliment him on his voice?" And you could never let Pat McCormack have access to a phone or else he would start calling up talk radio stations and prank them live on the air.

> **JONATHAN WINTERS**
>
> Feb 12 - 1964
>
> Dear Johnny —
> Got your card today — it was so good to hear from you and I can't begin to tell you how happy I am for you and your "bride" and your new nest. Many things — good things are happening at long last. The end of this month I'll know whether I made the first 5 for Best Supporting Actor and the Academy Award. As of now I'm in the top 10 which in itself is a big break. There's a good chance I'll be doing "Ship of Fools" for Stanley Kramer and have also been promised a good part in Hendersonville which he'll be doing next year. Eileen and the children are fine. We talk about you often and miss you more than you know. You're such a great talent — my only wish is that we could have more time together — But I hope to be on the Coast in a month or so and we'll get together then —
> Love to you both —
> Jonathan

One night during one of our parties, the alarm over at the home of our neighbor Sammy Davis Jr. unexpectedly went off. Sammy happened to be out of town at the time and was letting Sean Connery stay there in his absence. All of us at the party went outside to see what the commotion was all about. Suddenly, Sean bursts out of the house half dressed, waving a gun around, attempting to locate the perpetrators who tripped the alarm. At that very moment, the police showed up. Now, I'm guessing the police probably thought they had somehow wandered onto the set of a new James Bond film!

Not all parties took place at our house. Tim Conway would frequently have specialty parties. One time he rented a skating rink and required all of us to skate drunk. As you can imagine, it was complete mayhem, with one body after another sliding across the ice. Of course, no such event could begin without the proper opening ceremonies. It was therefore John's job to lead everyone in the singing of the national anthem, both American and Canadian (the Canadian version was for the benefit of our Canadian friends Ron Clark, a well known comedy writer, and his wife Sheila).

Sharing a laugh with our good friends Stella Atkinson and Ron & Sheila Clark

John had worked with the legendary singer and band leader Rudy Vallee during the filming of *How To Succeed In Business Without Really Trying*, and he and his wife Eleanor had become good friends of ours. They had a beautiful home at the top of the mountain that overlooked the entire valley, as well as private tennis courts. Rudy would have parties where we were all encouraged to play drunk tennis, with predictably hysterical results.

Throughout the years, I've had the pleasure of meeting nearly all of the Hollywood stars from the classic era. I was there when John Wayne stepped out of his dressing room one afternoon. He was huge! Harry Belafonte once greeted me by exclaiming, "Joan, you are gorgeous!" I responded by saying, "So are you!" And I will never forget meeting Burt Lancaster. Now there was a movie star! He was the most electrifyingly handsome man I think I have ever met. I just wanted to melt. The stars of the classic era were real stars. They all had a unique quality about them, unlike today where everybody's pretty much the same. Having said that, there are a few actors around today who I feel have that intangible magical something, such as Brad Pitt, George Clooney and Jennifer Lawrence.

ROBERT RYAN

Dear Jack –

Many thanks to you and Joan for the wire that came to Boston. It was a bright spot in a dark hour and I am most grateful.

The show is actually pretty bad but will run a long time. My singing has been compared favorably to Lincoln's but not to Tibbett's.
If ʸᵒᵘ get back to Gay Broadway I hope you'll drop by and say hello.

fondly

I will always remember a moment I shared with actor Robert Ryan. Bob had starred in a number of major films including *The Dirty Dozen, The Wild Bunch* and *The Longest Day* (along with Rod and just abut every other actor in Hollywood). He had invited John and me to join him on his boat for the day. At one point, I was lying down in the cabin below deck, when suddenly Bob opened the door ... and paused. Looking down, all he could see was this young bikini-clad actress lying across his bed bathed in the sunlight streaming through the open door. And looking up, all I could see was this stunningly handsome actor silhouetted against an orange and blue late afternoon sky. We both stared at each other for a few moments, and then simultaneously burst out in laughter. The irony of that moment was not lost ... we had each seen this same scene in countless romantic movies before.

John in Anthony and Cleopatra *at the Shakespeare Theatre in Stratford, CT*

John and I had met Bob Ryan years earlier while I was still doing *Candid Camera*. John was appearing opposite Katharine Hepburn and Bob in Shakespeare's *Anthony and Cleopatra* in Stratford, Connecticut. John of course was always playing practical jokes on everyone and would frequently do imitations of Bob, Kate and the other actors playing their respective roles. Often these actors would have a hard time keeping a straight face when doing scenes with John. Needless to say, Shakespeare was never the same again after John got through with it.

Learning to play tennis in Stratford while John was off doing Shakespeare.

Nelson Eddy was a famous entertainer who had become the highest paid singer in the world at one point during his career. One night, Nelson was appearing at a big hotel in L.A. and invited John and I to see the show. Afterwards, Nelson invited us up to his suite, which may have been a mistake. John ended up spending the entire evening discussing the importance and proper usage of the "u" vowel. And then Nelson would jump in and make corrections. It was hysterical.

Another hilarious incident took place at the home of Charlton Heston over on Coldwater Canyon. Chuck was appearing with John in a stage version of *A Man For All Seasons* at the Valley Music Theater, and he had invited the two of us over for drinks. I happened to be lying out by the pool. As Chuck exited the house and stepped onto the patio, he began to eye my sexy new polka dot bikini. Unfortunately, he stared a bit too long and lost sight of

John and me in our study at Evanview

where he was headed. All at once, he tripped over his own statue of Ben Hur, which sent the tray of glasses he was carrying, and himself, crashing to the deck.

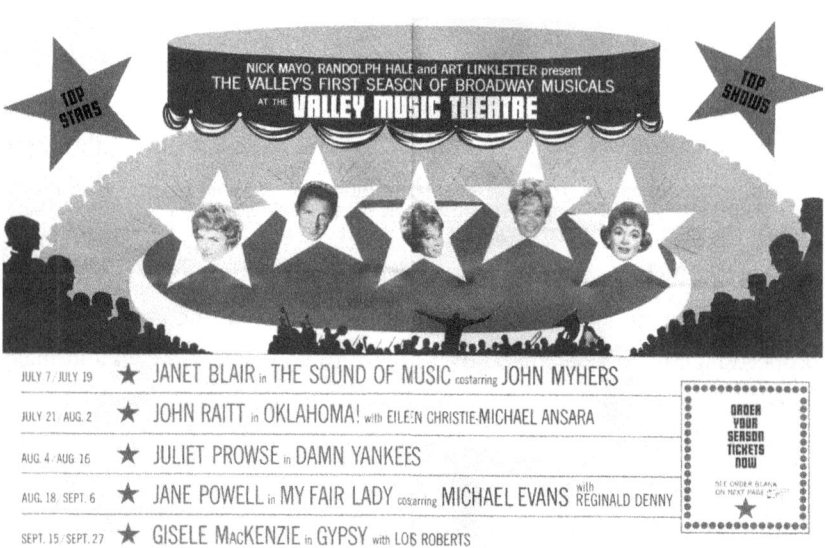

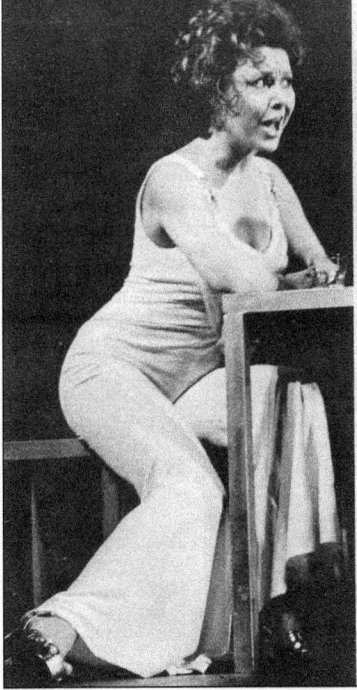

JOHN MYHERS DIRECTS "PROMISES"

Joan Benedict
as
Marge Mac Dougall

"PROMISES, PROMISES" AS PRESENTED AT THE UNION PLAZA IS BETTER THAN BROADWAY'S. CREDIT GOES TO THE SKILLFUL PRUNING BY DIRECTOR JOHN MYHERS, WHO DOUBLES AND SHOWS FURTHER EXCELLENCE IN HIS PORTRAYAL OF "DR. DRYFUSS".
FORREST DUKE, VARIETY

NONE OF THE IMPACT IS MISSING UNDER JOHN MYHERS' ABLE DIRECTION. MYHERS DEMONSTRATES HIS COMEDIC SKILL IN THE ROLE OF DR. DRYFUSS.
HAL BATES, L.A. HERALD EXAMINER

WHAT MAKES THE UNION PLAZA PRESENTATION SO SPECIAL IS . . . THERE COULDN'T BE A BETTER CAST, AND JOHN MYHERS TO DIRECT AND NEARLY STEAL THE SHOW AS DR. DRYFUSS.
JOE DELANEY, LAS VEGAS SUN

JOAN BENEDICT, A TALENTED LOOKER, DOES A MEMORABLE TIPSY BIT NEAR SHOW'S FINALE.
FORREST DUKE, VARIETY

JOHN MYHERS' MOST SERIOUS COMPETITION COMES FROM MRS. MYHERS, JOAN BENEDICT, AS THE LOVELY LADY LUSH.
JOE DELANEY, LAS VEGAS SUN

JOAN BENEDICT IN HER OWL FEATHERS IS ONE OF THE COMEDY HIGH POINTS OF THE UNION PLAZA'S "PROMISES, PROMISES".
TRUDY GILLETT, LAS VEGAS PANORAMA

THE TIGHT, FAST-MOVING DIRECTION REFLECTS THE TRIPLE TALENTS OF JOHN MYHERS, ACTOR-WRITER-DIRECTOR. HE KNOWS THE SCORE FROM BOTH SIDES OF THE FOOTLIGHTS.
RAOUL GRIPENWALDT, UNITED WESTERN NEWSPAPERS

The Valley Music Theater was a unique dome-shaped theater-in-the-round built during the mid-sixties in Woodland Hills, California, that had been financed by Bob Hope, Art Linkletter, Cy Warner and television producer Nick Mayo. John was chosen to open the theater with a version of *The Sound of Music* he was currently directing that starred Nick's wife, Janet Blair opposite John. The production was a huge success and John would go on to direct more than fifty musicals and stage plays during the course of his

career. John even directed me in a very successful version of *Promises, Promises* in Las Vegas where I received rave reviews portraying the always tipsy Margie MacDougall character.

Promises, Promises was the only musical I ever did. The dancing and singing instruction I had received years earlier provided me with a solid foundation. John did teach me a lot during that project, including the importance of how much distance there should be between actors on stage. But after he had seen me perform in *East of Eden*, he acknowledged that I didn't really need any direction. Years later, I ran into a girl in my tap class who had appeared in the chorus of *Promises, Promises* and asked her what she thought of the director. She responded, "Oh, I loved him! I thought he was great," not realizing that John was my husband.

Joan Benedict

as
Marge MacDougall

in
"Promises, Promises"

"...Joan Benedict as Marge MacDougall is unbelievably good. She is talented, beautiful, and totally smashed. Her scene with Chuck, 'A Fact Can Be,' is a show stopper."
Bernard Weiner, the Register

"...Joan Benedict played a female souse to perfection."
Ted Krec, Orange County Evening News

"...Joan Benedict created a masterpiece out of the role of Marge MacDougall."
John Yench, Anaheim Bulletin

"...'Promises, Promises' a rave review, especially Joan Benedict as the tipsy Marge MacDougall."
Sandra Lowell, LA Times

ORANGE PLAYHOUSE
DIRECTED BY JOHN MYHERS

IFA
BARRY FREED
THEATRE

DOROTHY DAY OTIS
COMMERCIALS

My wonderful John

The fact is everybody loved John. He was larger than life and had a very big personality. With John, it was all about music and comedy. He was funny *and* had this phenomenal voice. He could write and direct. He was a true renaissance man. Agents would often get confused when it came to booking him and wonder whether he was supposed to be a comedian, a singer, an actor, a writer or a director. Renaissance men are more accepted today. But back then, being too talented sometimes posed a problem.

One day we were in the bathroom and John said to me, "Come here and take a look at this." He opened his mouth and I could see a small spot on the back of his tongue. I took him to the dentist who immediately sent us to a nearby doctor. It's so strange how your world can change in an instant. One minute everything is great, and the next . . .

John was diagnosed with cancer of the tongue. For the next eight years, he became the guinea pig of doctors all over Southern California. They shot him so full of radiation. They tried everything they could think of. He was in and out of countless hospitals. It was horrible. One doctor in Encino even wanted to put John to sleep. I said, "No way," and took him back home with me where he held on for another six months. John had started out at 6' 2" and over 200 pounds. And by the end of the ordeal, he had withered away to 110 pounds.

They had taken away his amazing voice. He couldn't sing or talk, but he could still write scripts, which he did up until the very end. Finally, one morning he let me know that he was ready. I drove him to Cedars-Sinai Medical Center, and he quietly left us that afternoon. To this day, I miss him dearly. There was no one like John . . .

Chapter 11

In the Heat of the Moment

Yes, there was so much about John that I missed ... his sense of humor, his amazing voice, his incredible warmth and his love. We were married for thirty years and I had planned on spending the rest of my life with him. But now, that was no longer an option. The idea of dating again seemed so foreign to me after all this time. But I couldn't picture myself being alone.

Soon thereafter, I booked a trip to London just to get away and registered at the Dorchester Hotel. I immediately went into the suite, laid down on the bed and cried for nearly two hours.

On the return flight, I was sitting in first class when a good looking man sat down next to me. I said to him, "You're a pilot, aren't you?" He was dumbfounded, for he wasn't wearing a uniform. "How did you know?" he asked. I explained, "You just look like a pilot." As it turned out, he was on his way back to L.A. just like I was. Larry and I talked during the entire eight hour flight home. Luckily for me, he wasn't married. Larry invited me to dinner and we ended up seeing each other *over the next four years!*

One day, I mentioned to him that I had always wanted to fly a plane and before I knew it, he had arranged flying lessons for me at the Santa Monica Airport. Even though I was unable to eventually pass the ground school exam which was needed to get my license (you have to almost be an engineer to pass it, and I failed math in school), I did manage to have a great time flying high in my Cessna 172 for almost a year.

Learning to fly a Cessna 172

Although Larry was quite nice, we never really connected because I don't think he could understand or relate to someone who had a passion for the arts. It was clear that if I was going to find a man, he would probably have to be an actor, or a musician, or at least someone from the entertainment industry. I've always loved creative people and still do.

And then it happened. One day I got a call out of the blue. The voice on the other end asked, "Joan?" I was instantly taken aback. He continued, "Joan, this is Rod Steiger." Even though Rod and I hadn't seen each other in years, I immediately recognized his voice. There was no possible way this could be a joke, for how could anyone duplicate that unmistakable voice with such precision. "Rod," I countered, "how on earth did you find me?" His response was classic: "Joan . . . I'm Rod Steiger."

Joan . . . I'm Rod Steiger

You may recall Rod and I had met in New York many years earlier, before I had married John, on a television program I was doing called *Masquerade Party*. It was a show that featured a different celebrity guest each week appearing in various vignettes wearing a mask. It was the job of the panelists (and the audience) to try and figure out the identity of the celebrity during the course of the program. At the end of the show the celebrity guest would remove the mask to the delight of the viewers. The script for this particular episode called for me to dance with Rod, and I was excited to say the least.

This would be my very first time appearing opposite a really big Hollywood star.

Rod and I dancing on Masquerade Party

Over the years I have been asked repeatedly what it's like to work with a famous actor. I always tell people that it's really quite easy . . . as long as the actor is good. It's just like playing tennis: The more experienced your opponent, the better you yourself are able to play.

We were about twenty minutes away from going on air. I was in the final stages of make up. Suddenly I heard a voice from across the room call out to me. "Come here, little girl." I turned to see Rod standing in the doorway. In those days he had a full head of dark wavy hair. A couple of years earlier, while filming a movie called *The Big Knife*, the studio insisted he bleach his hair for the role. Rod always believed the harsh chemicals that were used on set during filming contributed to his eventual hair loss. Speaking of studios, they were always on his case to lose weight. They wanted to mold him into a leading man à la James Dean or Tony Curtis. But Rod ignored their requests. He preferred the meatier roles that would eventually become his trademark.

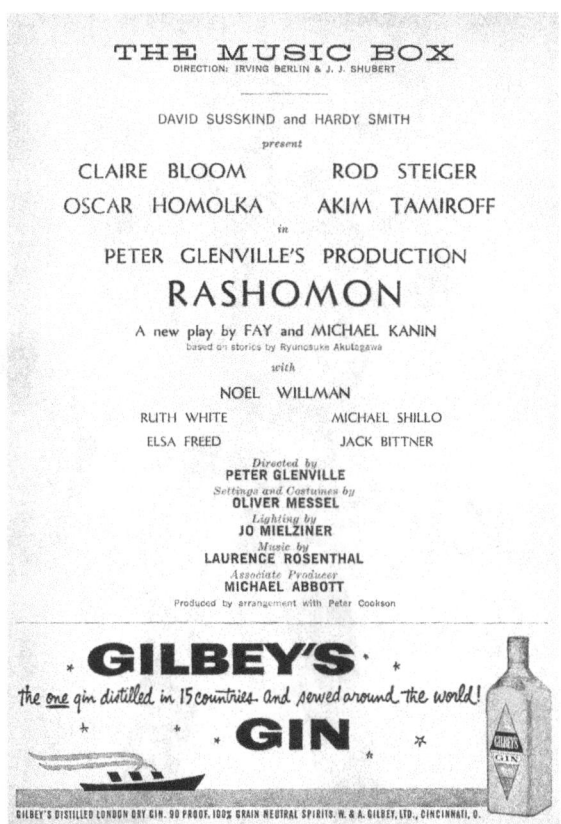

The conversation we had that evening in the make up room resulted in him asking me out to dinner, along with an invitation to see him in the Broadway play *Rashomon*. For Rod to be appearing in a play was quite unusual. I later learned that he was very uncomfortable on stage and instead preferred working in film and television. Nevertheless, Rod, always the professional, never let his discomfort show and the play wound up receiving three Tony Award nominations during its six month run on Broadway.

As we crossed Broadway toward the Chinese restaurant that would serve as the location of our first date, we passed by a huge theater marquee advertising the newly released film *Al Capone*, which happened to star Rod Steiger in the title role. Believe it or not, Rod had to be coaxed into taking the role since he hated the gangster with a passion. Yet ultimately, Rod agreed to

do the film and was able to transcend his own prejudices and deliver a truly frightening and convincing performance.

Seeing Rod standing there right in front of me, smiling, with the marquee spelling out his name behind him was a vividly surreal moment that I remember to this day. It was then that it really hit me: I was on a date with one of the biggest Hollywood celebrities in the business. Film, television, stage— Rod could do it all.

Rod Steiger as Al Capone

After ordering our food, we talked for a few minutes. Then Rod took some notes from his pocket and asked if I'd like to hear some of his poetry. I was instantly taken aback. What? Rod Steiger . . . a poet? Wait . . . what?

All of his roles up to that point had me convinced that he was mister tough guy. But Rod Steiger, a writer of poetry? I had to quickly juxtapose my thinking process in order to wrap my head around this. "Sure, I'd love to hear what you've written," I stammered. Here was this man who was appearing right across the street at the local movie theater as the notorious gangster Al Capone about to read me his poetry! Rod said he had been writing little poems ever since he was a young boy. He began reading and I instantly began to see the real Rod . . . a sweet, sensitive, gentle and very caring man, which were all the qualities I adored. Incidentally, I still have all of his poems.

He was born of love
And therefore,
Stood frozen and amazed
At the absence of warmth
Around him-
Seeking a God that could explain
Caring
Questioning
Dauntless
Daring
Always anxious
As he could feel the warmth
He was given
Slip from his soul-
And the calcification
Of self-manufactured hope
Swamp his being
Cutting off
Any flames of compassion-
He died
In exasperation
A victim of his new-found
Civilisation.

Romance does not die with age
Dreams
Have ever-expanding dimensions-

If in the heart of the aging being
The thrill of challenge remains
So does the need for participation.
The love of the combat of living
The prodding of desire
Carries no calenders.

To withdraw from the continuous struggle
Is to kiss Death full on the mouth

Poems of Rod Steiger

He had given me a glimpse inside the real Rod. He was friendly, conversational and had many close friends. But as far as the public was concerned, he was a mean, tough, bad ass villain. Frequently when we would be out in public, fans wouldn't dare approach him but would instead quietly ask me if Rod would be willing to sign an autograph. Some were afraid he'd get angry; maybe even try and kill them! Would these fans believe that his real dreams included wanting to become a singer and a stand up comedian? It's true! Yes indeed, Rod was a great actor and a pussycat rolled into one. We talked the night away and continued to see each other.

Rod made his film debut in the 1951 film *Teresa* where he had a small role as a psychiatrist. However, his first real film was 1954's *On The Waterfront* where he starred opposite Marlon Brando. Rod received his first Academy Award nomination for his portrayal of Charley Malloy, the brother of Brando's character.

Marlon was a bad boy and tried to out-improvise Rod during filming. But Rod was a master and easily held his own. While Rod was very encouraging on the set, helping the other actors to do their best work, Marlon was just the opposite. He refused to stick around for the shooting of any scenes involving reverse angles, which put an unnecessary hardship on the other actors.

Teresa, *Rod's motion picture debut*

The famous scene between Steiger and Brando in On The Waterfront

Years later, after Rod and I were together, we met with Marlon for dinner at a local Chinese restaurant. Throughout the evening, Marlon was very complimentary toward Rod. Both had plenty to talk about and the evening ended on a high note. Unfortunately, it would be the last time these two legends would ever reminisce together.

Like a lot of young men, Rod was initially motivated to get into acting as a way to score girls. However, he quickly became very adept at his craft and excelled in whatever part came his way. Soon he was taking roles based on the artistry of the script rather than the potential paycheck. He became particularly enamored with biographies, choosing films which allowed him to play such diverse characters as Al Capone (1959), Napoleon Bonaparte (1970), W.C. Fields (1976) and Pontius Pilate (1977).

One of Rod's earliest films was the hit musical *Oklahoma*, and he was petrified of having to do it. He had made a request of the studio to find a "dance double" for him. He was afraid that he would drop his dance partner Bambi Linn during one of the many lifts he was required to do. Famous choreographer Agnes de Mille called Rod into her office just before shooting was to begin and told him that they had indeed found an actor to do his dance sequences for him. Relieved and excited, Rod exclaimed, "Great! Who?" to which Agnes replied, "You!" Rod nearly fainted. Yet ultimately, he was able to pull it off. So whenever you watch *Oklahoma*, just remember, that really is Rod doing all of his own singing and dancing... and no doubt trying hard to impress co-star Shirley Jones whom he had the hots for!

Another notable film of Rod's was *The Harder They Fall* in which he starred opposite Humphrey Bogart. This would turn out to be Bogart's last film. At one point during production, Bogart turned to director Mark Robson and complained, "Hey, this kid's killing me," in reference to Rod's strong ability as an actor. Bogart was afraid that Rod might overshadow his performance in the final edit of the film.

Now, it is generally agreed that among Rod's massive body of work his greatest film performance was that of Sol Nazerman in 1965's *The Pawnbroker*. Likewise, it was universally assumed that Rod would be walking away with

Rod as Napoleon Bonaparte in Waterloo

Rod as W. C. Fields in W. C. Fields And Me

Rod with Gordon MacRae in Oklahoma

Rod and Humphrey Bogart in a scene from The Harder They Fall

the Best Actor statue at that year's Academy Awards ceremony. However, when Lee Marvin's name was announced instead, you could hear an audible gasp from the assembled audience.

Rod was understandably surprised and disappointed. However, he was vindicated two years later when he received the Best Actor award from the Academy for his portrayal of Sheriff Bill Gillespie in Norman Jewison's *In The Heat Of The Night*. Co-star Sydney Poitier considered Rod to be a genius.

Rod in The Pawnbroker

Rod with In The Heat Of The Night *co-star Sidney Poitier*

Rod discusses a scene with In The Heat Of The Night *director Norman Jewison*

Sitting with Rod's Best Actor Oscar

My own personal favorite of Rod's is *Dr. Zhivago* where he played the villain Victor Komarovsky. Rod would always proudly point out that he was the only American cast member in that film. Yet, despite his many successes in Hollywood, Rod never got over the fact that he made a big mistake in turning down the role of *Patton*, a role which won George C. Scott an Oscar for Best Actor and ultimately put Scott on the map.

Rod with Julie Christie in a scene from Dr. Zhivago

Our courtship back in New York during the spring of 1959 turned out to be short lived. Rod's schedule took him to Hollywood and I would begin dating John Myhers, my soon to be husband. We ended up going our separate ways. But here we were thirty-eight years later on the phone, talking as if time had stood still. We made a decision to get together, and incredibly, we were able to pick up right where we left off. I had always been a fan of Rod's and found him to be smart, talented, considerate, generous and sexy.

Me and Rod

The year was now 1997. Rod and I had become a couple, and life was about to get even crazier...

My beautiful Rod

Chapter 12

The End of an Era

During the mid-1990s, a trivia game known as The Six Degrees of Kevin Bacon began to weave its way into America's consciousness. It was based on a concept known as the "six degrees of separation" which suggests that any two individuals on Earth can be linked together via six or less acquaintances. By utilizing mathematics and applying the rules to the entertainment industry, the game's experts determined that Rod Steiger himself was the most "linkable" actor in the business, which promptly earned Rod the title of "Center of the Hollywood Universe."

As soon as we rekindled our romance, Rod began spoiling me, placing me at the center of his universe. We traveled the world, stayed at the nicest hotels and dined at the finest restaurants. If I happened to see something in a shop that I liked, he would instantly buy it for me. Every day he would write me poetry, little love notes, and bring me roses. Every day! Can you believe it? Our love flourished.

One of the first projects Rod did after we had gotten back together was a small Canadian film called *The Kid*, a boxing movie with a similar theme to that of his earlier triumph *The Harder They Fall*. This was followed by two more boxing themed films: *Body & Soul* and another which re-teamed Rod with his *In the Heat of the Night* director Norman Jewison. Titled *The Hurricane*, this critically acclaimed bio-pic featured Denzel Washington as a boxer accused of a triple murder and Rod as a conflicted southern judge. Not surprisingly, I soon found myself getting interested in boxing and always joined Rod in watching the big matches, which of course made him quite happy.

Rod and me on the set of Body & Soul

On the set of Body & Soul *with Ray "Boom Boom" Mancini*

At the Toronto Film Festival with Rod and In the Heat of the Night *director Norman Jewison*

That same year, Rod appeared opposite Melanie Griffin in the Antonio Banderas directed film *Crazy in Alabama*. Once again, Rod played a judge in this highly rated, well made film. During the production, we became friends with Antonio and Melanie and would often be invited over to their house. At the time, it was obvious that Antonio absolutely adored his wife. Our friend Robert Wagner, who also appeared in the film, was a frequent dinner guest with all of us. I had previously worked with RJ on the series *The Trials of Rosie O'Neill* and we all got along wonderfully. As a side note, I was well aware that Melanie's mom, actress Tippi Hedren, had a thing for Rod.

In 1998, Rod put aside his dislike of awards ceremonies and took me to the Academy Awards. They had a reunion of previous Best Actor and Actress winners that year and he was asked to attend. It was an amazing experience to mingle among seven decades worth of legendary stars. At one point, I saw an elderly woman standing around and thought it might be Roddy McDowell's grandmother. It turned out to be Luise Rainer, the first woman ever to win two consecutive Best Actress Oscars.

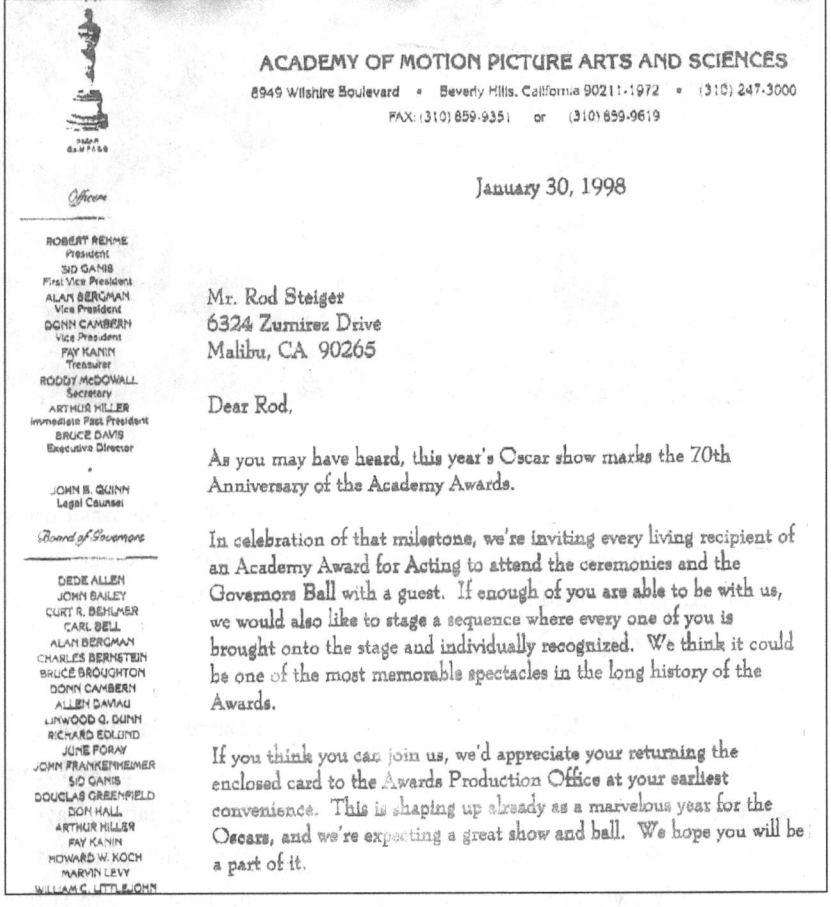

Rod had been friends with Elizabeth Taylor for quite a long time and it was expected that he would be taking her to the Academy Awards ceremony. When he made the decision to take me instead, Liz called up and asked him to change his mind. When Rod confirmed that he would be taking me, she suggested that the three of us go together. Rod told her that wasn't an option. Of course, the tabloids had a field day with all of this. But it didn't end there.

A few months later, Rod got in contact with his friend Liz regarding a script he had written. It was an updated version of *The Wizard Of Oz* and

All of the Best Actor and Actress winners assembled together on one stage

he wondered if she might be interested in one of the roles. This was during one of her "down" periods, and Rod had hoped he could encourage her to return to acting. He called her to set up a lunch date so that they could meet and discuss the project. Naturally, the paparazzi surrounded the area and documented the encounter.

Later that week, Rod and I were on our way to Barcelona. As we took our seats on the plane, I noticed a National Enquirer nearby. I picked it up and turned it over. The headline read, "Rod Steiger to Wed Elizabeth Taylor!" I held it up for Rod to see and awaited his response. In an attempt to diffuse the humorously awkward situation, he simply offered, "Joan . . . I'm sitting right here!"

Regardless, the tabloids continued to assume that Rod and Liz were dating. And apparently, so did Liz. So when Rod asked me to marry him, the tabloids went into overdrive. I have a copy of the Enquirer showing Liz in tears because she had somehow lost Rod to me. Liz even called me up and asked how it all could have happened. I told her that Rod had simply proposed to me and I accepted. She didn't realize at the time that I was the same Joan Benedict who had worked with her on *Butterfield 8*. I thought

Sad, lonely and pain-racked Liz lets Steiger go

Tormented by pain, Liz Taylor has made the ultimate sacrifice — she's dumped beloved beau Rod Steiger for his own good.

And now the anguished actress is resigned to living out her twilight years all alone.

The tragic star cut loose her devoted 73-year-old boyfriend after breaking her back in February — and she's become heartsick as the Oscar-winning actor kicks up his heels with former "General Hospital" star Joan Benedict.

"Sometimes I wonder which is worse — the pain in my back, or the pain in my heart," Liz told a friend. "But I had no choice but to let Rod go."

Liz' friend said: "Rod

By MICHAEL GLYNN

swept her off her feet and the love between them grew quickly. Rod wasn't looking for anything from Liz and vice versa. They just enjoyed each other's company.

"But just when happiness was at hand, cruel fate pulled the rug out from under Liz. Her joy crumbled after the fall in February that makes it difficult for her to walk. Rod was willing to stick by Liz' side but she didn't want Rod to be tied to her with all her problems right now."

A devastated Liz, 66, told her pal, "Letting go of Rod was one of the hardest things I've ever had to do.

"Our feelings for each other were just beginning to grow and he was making me so happy. But I had to face facts. How could Rod and I go on together with me this way, trapped here because of my back? It just wouldn't be fair to him.

about writing her a note explaining that to her, but never got around to it. So she never knew.

For thirty years, Rod had owned a beautiful beach house on Malibu Road in Malibu. However, when we reunited, he sold that house and purchased a beautiful home in the Malibu hills on three acres overlooking the ocean. We had our wedding there which was just fabulous. All of our friends, including various agents and actors came, including James Garner.

We had the back deck completely lined with white roses. My daughter Claudia was the bridesmaid. The judge who presided over the ceremony

The view from our house overlooking Malibu

happened to be named Merrick, the same name as the town in Long Island where I grew up. Of course, the paparazzi were waiting for us at the end of the driveway. Afterwards, we all went to Taverna Tony's in Malibu for a lively reception which lasted well into the night.

Mr. and Mrs. Rod Steiger with Judge Merrick

Within days, we began an extended honeymoon that took us all over the world... Paris, Manila, Rome, Istanbul. We stayed at some amazing hotels in Switzerland which had such incredible views. He would take me to beautiful museums and art galleries (Rod had always been an avid art collector). He would even sing to me in the car. We just had so much fun together.

Honeymooning in Paris

Rod and me at the grave of Vincent Van Gogh and his brother Theo outside Paris

Me at the Blue Mosque in Istanbul, Turkey

The view from our Honeymoon Suite, the former Ciragan Palace which is now a hotel in Istanbul, overlooking the Bosphorus River

We also traveled to Monte Carlo to see Rod's daughter, famed opera singer Anna Steiger, perform. She was the daughter he had had with his second wife Claire Bloom. Anna loved me and introduced me to the cast at one of her performances as her stepmother. I thought that was lovely.

And the magic just kept going. Rod wanted me to experience the finest things that life had to offer. We were dinner guests of the mayor in Athens and guests at the king's palace in Spain. When we would check into a five star hotel he would always get us the biggest suite. And as we would enter the room, he would say, "Does this suit Madame?" and then laugh heartily as only he could. Rod was the most loving and generous man you could ever meet.

One time we were in one of the holding rooms at the Venice Film Festival having cocktails when suddenly we were notified that it was our turn to walk the red carpet. We opened the door to thousands of cheering fans all chanting, "Rod! Rod!" He was such an icon over in Europe. The red carpet was about two blocks long with throngs of people lining both sides. As we walked toward the theater, we were being videotaped, which was simultaneously being projected onto a huge overhead screen. Once inside, I was seated next to Rod on one side and French heartthrob Alain Delon on the other. How lucky can a girl get?

Rod then arranged to take me to the Kentucky Derby. He had previously served as the race's Grand Marshall back in the early 1970s. Now, everybody knows the race is really just an excuse to attend a lot of parties. We were there with Richard Dreyfuss. While waiting for the race to start, some scantily clad woman came up to Rod, threw her arms around him and sat down in his lap, right in front of me. Taken aback, Rod quickly introduced me to this nubile young thing, but she didn't seem to care. Richard thought it was funny. I'm not so sure I did.

Soon thereafter, we attended the Super Bowl in New Orleans as guests of the owner of the St. Louis Rams. That year, the Rams were pitted against the New England Patriots. It was an exciting game and we had a fabulous time. Afterwards, we tried to find our way back to the limo and got lost. The stadium was something like ten city blocks long. We never did find the car and had to ask one of the cleaning men to give us a ride back to the hotel.

Another trip I will never forget involved traveling to Ireland to attend the wedding of our dear friends Pierce and Keely Brosnan. Pierce had co-starred with Rod in the off-the-wall science fiction film *Mars Attacks* and the two had been neighbors in Malibu for years. I believe Rod and I were the only celebrities who attended the wedding. It was held at the beautiful Ballintubber Abbey in County Mayo in Western Ireland.

Rod and me at the wedding of Pierce and Keely Brosnan in Ireland

Afterwards, we stayed at the magnificent Ashford Castle and watched the fireworks as they reflected off the castle's lake. The festivities extended well into the early hours of the morning. It was so heartwarming to see Pierce happy again following the tragic loss of his first wife.

Whenever Rod got sent a script, he would ask me to read it and then say, "Have you picked out your part yet?" I never asked him or pressured him to do that. He just had confidence in me. Rod was my biggest champion and would always tell reporters I was a great actress. We ended up doing two films together, both in 2001. The first was called *The Flying Dutchman* which we shot in Montana. They later changed the name of the film to *Frozen In Fear*, but I prefer the original title.

Rod and me on location in Montana

Me and my Flying Dutchman *co-star Eric Roberts*

The film starred Rod and me alongside our friend Eric Roberts, who is an excellent actor. I played Rod's sister in the film, a woman named Moira who runs a motel. We shared an incredibly intense scene together where I'm supposed to be playing solitaire and Rod comes in and confronts me. Rod had me improvise the scene with him and after it was over, the entire crew erupted in applause. The director was so impressed, they wrote a couple of extra scenes for me. I therefore had to stay on in Montana an extra two weeks while Rod returned to Malibu for a previously arranged interview.

The other film we did together was a tear-jerker titled *A Month of Sundays* and featured Rod and me opposite Sally Kirkland and Michael Paré. In the film I played Dr. Stanz, Rod's doctor. I have some good scenes in that film as well. During the shoot, Rod arranged an "awards ceremony" just for me in front of the entire crew and presented me with an "Oscar" with my name inscribed on it. It was very sweet of him to do that, and a little embarrassing. But I loved working with Rod. He always made me feel like I could do anything.

Me with A Month of Sundays *co-star Sally Kirkland*

To let off steam midweek, Rod would play poker every Wednesday night when he wasn't working. The games were at the home of his agent in Beverly Hills and were always frequented by a number of celebrities including Martin Landau, Sharon Stone, Charles Durning, Eric Roberts, and Mimi Rogers. Rod would usually lose since he didn't have a poker face, while Eric would lament as to why the press always referred to Emma Roberts as Julia Roberts' niece rather than his daughter. Afterwards, Rod never felt like driving back to Malibu. So we usually spent the night at the Bel Air Hotel in Beverly Hills.

Poker Night with the gang. Standing L to R: Rod, James Farentino, Eric Roberts, Charles Durning, George Dzundza, Martin Landau. Sitting L to R: Agent Norby Walters, Mimi Rogers, Kevin Pollack, Sharon Stone

One of Rod's last films was a comedy titled *The Hollywood Sign* which also starred Burt Reynolds and Tom Berenger. Burt thought Rod was the greatest, and I found Burt to be very charming, a true gentleman. After a long day's shoot, the cast would all go to the Saddle Peak Lodge in Calabasas for dinner. We had a wonderful time.

Rod's 75th birthday celebration

Rod's 75th birthday celebration with James Garner and my daughter Claudia

Rod's 75th birthday celebration with Burt Reynolds and Jonathan Winters

Rod's 75th birthday celebration with Jonathan Winters and me

Rod and me on the set of The Hollywood Sign

Rod and me with Burt Reynolds

Rod with Burt Reynolds and Tom Berenger after a long day on the set of The Hollywood Sign

Rod and me with Burt and Tom

Rod receives his star on the Hollywood Walk of Fame

Rod with Luciano Pavarotti and Frank Sinatra

February 23, 2000

Rod and Joanie Steiger
C/o Lori De Waal
7080 Hollywood Blvd # 515
Los Angeles, CA 90028

Dear Rod and Joanie:

The Society of Singers gala was a night I will always remember as a very special occasion. I wanted to thank you for your help in making the evening so wonderful and all of your support and good wishes through the years.

Sincerely,

Tony Bennett

Rod and me with Carrie Fisher

Rod and me with Chad Everett

Rod and me with Marvel Comic's Stan Lee

Rod with Annette Bening

Rod and me with Charlton Heston honoring Ray Bradbury

Rod and Ray Bradbury

One day, Ann-Margret showed up on the *Hollywood Sign* set, immediately walked over to Rod and bowed down before him. Most of the crew, many of whom weren't even born when Rod first appeared on the scene, were in awe of Rod. He was, after all, a legend. Even in his fifth decade of working in Hollywood, Rod continued to be revered by many for his tremendous talent and understanding of the artistry of acting.

During much of his career, Rod waged an inner battle against two different opponents: depression and food. Rod's struggle with depression had been well documented in the past. However, by the time he and I got together, he had found the proper medication to keep his illness under control. Never once did I see any evidence of depression in Rod during our marriage. But I did see him eat all the wrong foods.

In the summer of 2002, while we were getting ready to leave for Barcelona to do a movie, Rod suddenly fell ill and had to be rushed to the hospital. It was determined that he had a tiny trace of cancer on his pancreas. The question was, did we catch it in time? An operation was performed and was a success! As I had done with John, I remained with Rod at the hospital during his entire stay.

Just prior to his release from the hospital, Rod inadvertently received a dose of Toradol from an intern, which is a pain medication sometimes used after surgery to reduce swelling. However, Rod's charts clearly indicated that he was not to be given Toradol. His adverse reaction to the drug was immediate, and the staff quickly tried everything they could to revive him. But it was too late. My husband, the legendary Rod Steiger, was gone.

Once again, I was shocked, saddened and devastated beyond words. The official cause of death was listed as pneumonia and complications from surgery. A doctor friend of mine was able to obtain Rod's medical records and tried to convince me to sue the hospital, since he firmly believed they had killed him. But that kind of thing just wasn't for me. It was too negative and would have likely dragged on for years. And it wouldn't have brought Rod back.

JIMMY CARTER

July 12, 2002

To Joan Benedict Steiger

    We were saddened to learn of Rod's death. Please know you are in our hearts and prayers during this difficult time. We hope that your warm memories and the love and support of your family, friends, and the many people whose lives he touched will be of comfort to you in the days ahead.

                  Sincerely,

                  Jimmy Carter
                  Rosalynn Carter

Mrs. Rod Steiger
6324 Zumirez Drive
Malibu, California 90255

You are cordially invited to

A special tribute to the illustrious career of the late actor

ROD STEIGER

Guest speakers Norman Jewison, Jonathan Winters,
Scott Wilson, Joan Benedict Steiger

Sunday, May 2, 2004

Tribute and clip show – 5:30 p.m.

Presentation of newly established
Rod Steiger Scholarships in Acting at UCLA

Refreshments

Screening of THE PAWNBROKER – 7:00 p.m.

James Bridges Theater, UCLA Melnitz Hall

Complimentary Tickets – RSVP (310) 206-6154

Melnitz Hall is located on the northeast corner of the UCLA campus, near the intersection of Sunset Boulevard and Hilgard Avenue.

Parking is available for $7 at the gate of Parking Lot 3 adjacent to Melnitz Hall.

QUINCY JONES

July 18, 2002

Dear Joan,

This book was given to me by Alice Walker during an emotional time in my life. I wanted to share it with you in hopes you might find some solace in the gentle thoughts.

Please allow those who love and care for you to support you during this difficult time. Please call on me for anything I can do to make things easier.

♥ Quincy

ROD STEIGER'S SAD LAST DAYS

Steiger with his beloved fifth wife Joan

'I always liked playing tough guys, but this is just too much'

OSCAR winner Rod Steiger was in terrible pain during the sad final weeks of his life – but he endured it with grim humor, say insiders.

"Rod winced and said, 'I always liked playing tough guys...but this is getting a bit too much,'" reveals a source close to the actor. "Toward the end, the doctors mercifully gave him medication so that he could handle it.

"He slept for long periods and his passage was eased."

Suffering from severe stomach pains and digestive problems, Steiger was admitted to St. John's Medical Center in Santa work and he just wanted to continue."

Ironically, immediately after his surgery, Steiger's longtime publicist Lori DeWaal said, "Considering his age, Rod is doing amazingly well. He is scheduled to star in a film titled, The Row, in October, and they say he will be completely recovered by then."

But days later, Steiger took a turn for the worse – he contracted deadly pneumonia and his kidneys failed.

"There was nothing more the doctors could do at that point," says the friend.

"They could have dealt with the pneumonia by giv-

Steiger's Roar

When a role called for gutsy power, Rod Steiger was a sure contender

Rod Steiger was of the same Hollywood generation as Marlon Brando, James Dean and Monty Clift. Like them, he studied the Method approach to acting and, like them, wowed audiences with his emotional realism. What he lacked, with a face that looked as if it belonged in a crowd rather than on a screen, was sex appeal. "I missed that one prerequisite for real stardom," he once said. "If you don't get the female following of a tribe, you don't get that big."

The ladies got one less hunk, but Hollywood gained the Legend, as his friend Pierce Brosnan always called him. Steiger, who died at 77 on July 9 following surgery for an intestinal tumor, was powerful in role after role: a corrupt lawyer in 1954's *On the Waterfront*, for which he was nominated for a Supporting Actor Oscar; a bigoted sheriff in '67's *In the Heat of the Night*, which brought a Best Actor Oscar; a jealous farmhand (*Oklahoma!*); a Russian cad (*Doctor Zhivago*).

He vanished from movies in the '80s, crippled by a depression that led to three suicide attempts before he was treated with medication. "I have experienced the pain... the embarrassment," he said in 1994. That shared suffering was the basis for his friendship with Elizabeth Taylor, who was housebound by the illness in the 1990s. "I will miss his gruff tenderness and humor," Taylor says.

In his last few years Steiger—whose four previous wives included actress Claire Bloom—at last succeeded as a romantic lead. He wed actress Joan Benedict, 60, in 2000. "Every day he bought me roses—a huge bouquet," says Benedict. "He was so grateful he had finally found happiness." •

"I would have loved to be a singer," Steiger once said, "but they never would have shut me up."

In the classic *Waterfront* scene, Brando tells Steiger, "I coulda been a contender."

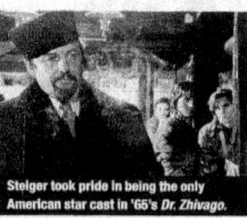
Steiger took pride in being the only American star cast in '65's *Dr. Zhivago*.

"We laughed together, dreamed together," says *Heat* costar Sidney Poitier.

I had lost another man I loved. My time with Rod had passed far too quickly. All of his friends came to the memorial including our new friend Burt Reynolds, as did the young boy who had appeared alongside Rod in the film *The Pawnbroker*. He was now all grown up and barely recognizable.

It was indeed the end of an era.

Chapter 13

Riding with Angels

FOUR YEARS HAD PASSED since my precious Rod had died. I was alone one evening watching television when the title of a film flashed across the screen. It read *Hell's Angel's '69*. The film starred Jeremy Slate, a handsome, blond, blue-eyed actor whom I had met back in New York when we were both just starting out. He was appearing on Broadway opposite Miriam Hopkins. He was married at the time but had since gotten divorced. I soon began to wonder whatever happened to him.

Before meeting in New York, Jeremy had been in the Navy and had coincidentally landed at Normandy at the same time as my first husband George. In his first two feature films, Jeremy was paired opposite Elvis Presley

Left: A young Jeremy Slate. Right: Jeremy with Elvis Presley in Girls! Girls! Girls!

Jeremy and co-star Keith Larson in The Aquanauts

in *G.I. Blues* and *Girls! Girls! Girls!* In between the two films he starred in his own TV series called *The Aquanauts* (later re-titled *Malibu Run*) and guested on a number of television programs including *Ozzie and Harriet, Have Gun – Will Travel, Perry Mason, The Untouchables, Dr. Kildare, Route 66,* and *Alfred Hitchcock Presents.*

Jeremy with Dennis Hopper in True Grit

Jeremy did a lot of westerns including *The Virginian, Bonanza* and *Gunsmoke,* along with the films *The Sons of Katie Elder* and *True Grit,* both starring John Wayne. Also featured in *True Grit* was Jeremy's friend Dennis Hopper. Dennis and Jeremy would often sneak off the set between takes and hide somewhere so they could smoke a joint. One time John Wayne himself went out looking for them and caught them red handed. Singer Glen Campbell appeared in the film as well and Jeremy would often write songs for him. Jeremy was an accomplished country western songwriter who had previously written the top ten Tex Ritter hit *Just Beyond the Moon.*

Jeremy would soon go on to star in a series of biker films for American International Pictures starting with *Born Losers,* which introduced the character of Billy Jack to the world. This was quickly followed by *The Mini-Skirt Mob, Hells Belles* and finally *Hells Angels '69,* which he also co-wrote. I consider this last film in the series to be one of Jeremy's finest performances. He actually broke his leg during the filming of the movie but managed to complete the shoot. Several real life Hell's Angels had parts in the film

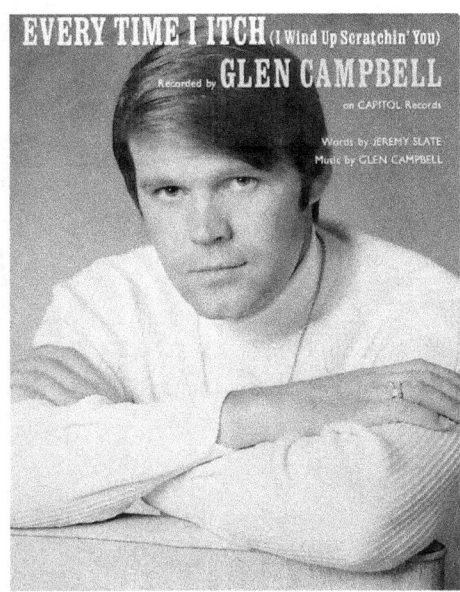

One of the songs Jeremy wrote for Glen Campbell

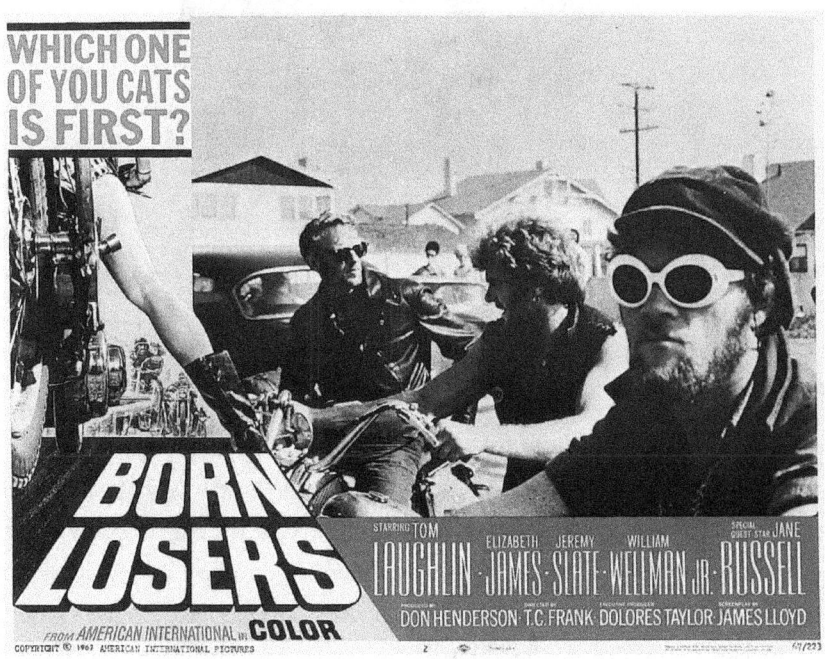

including club president Sonny Barger, which ultimately endeared Jeremy to the notorious motorcycle club from that point on.

After that, Jeremy was signed to a seven year contract with Paramount and also had a long running lead role on the soap opera *One Life to Live*. More television guest appearances followed including major parts on *The Man from UNCLE*, *Bewitched*, *Combat!*, *Tarzan*, *Mission: Impossible*, *Mannix*, and *Police Story*.

I'd heard that Jeremy's first wife had caught him fooling around and proceeded to set all his clothes on fire. Jeremy's response was simply, "Well, I guess that's it." He then married actress Tammy Grimes, but that only lasted a few months. So I called him up and was surprised to find that he was now semi-retired. His last film had been the 1992 thriller *Lawnmower Man* where he appeared opposite my friend Pierce Brosnan, after which he began living a very hippy life up in Monterey. He was now a "free spirit." Most of his friends in Monterey were hippies. The sign above his home read "funky heaven." We had a wonderful conversation on the phone and I made arrangements to fly up to see him.

The name for Jeremy's Monterey home

Our first meeting in Monterey

When I arrived at the Monterey airport, Jeremy claimed that "a wave of happiness swept over him," a phrase he would often repeat when we were enjoying wonderful moments together. He was just as handsome as ever with his long blond hair. I quickly learned that the reason he had given up his career was so that he could care for his son Jeff who had AIDS. Jeff had already passed by the time we got together. Yes, Jeremy was truly an angel and was very close with all of his children.

Jeremy asked me to move up to Monterey and I said I just couldn't do that. So he came down to Malibu to be with me and ended up staying for four years! I knew he must be in love with me because he left his cats behind, giving them to a friend in Monterey who was happy to look after them. Now that's real love!

Jeremy and me at The Cypress Inn in Carmel, CA; a pet friendly hotel owned by Doris Day

Jeremy was very easy to get along with. We would go to soap opera awards ceremonies and western film award shows. We just had a lot of great times together. With John, it had been all about music and comedy. With Rod, it had been about culture and art. And with Jeremy, well, it was all about sex. What can I say? It's true!

Left: Jeremy and me at the Soap Awards.
Right: Jeremy and me on our way to the Western Film Awards

Jeremy and me arriving at Graceland as special guests of the Elvis Presley Film Festival

Jeremy with our good friend Don Knotts

Like John and Rod before, Jeremy was very encouraging to me and my acting career. At the time, I was appearing in a wonderful play by Donald Marguiles called *Collected Stories* and Jeremy would come to see me every night. It was so incredible to have such support. A few years earlier, Rod had come to see me in the *Octette Bridge Club* but didn't tell me he was going to be in the audience for fear it would have made me nervous. Frankly, it wouldn't have. I've always felt very comfortable on stage and I believe the stage is where I've done some of my best work. Even though memorizing lines is difficult for me, I feel that acting in front of an audience can be far more authentic than on a movie set in front of a camera crew.

Just after John passed, I did the play *Leona* at the Matrix in Hollywood. It was a one woman show detailing the life of Leona Helmsley, the tyrannical business woman dubbed "the queen of mean" who eventually went to prison. It was a grueling one hour and twenty minutes on stage with no breaks. I really had to be prepared. In fact, I spent nearly six months rehearsing.

Jeremy and me with Collected Stories *director Carmen Milito*

Me as Leona, "the Queen of Mean"

the World Premiere of
LEONA
Written by BRENDA LILLY

starring
JOAN BENEDICT

"Joan Benedict is a vivid, compelling and convincing Leona Helmsley"
—Drama-Logue

**The Matrix Theatre
7657 Melrose Avenue
(213) 466-1767**

"Joan Benedict gives a tour de force performance as the dethroned monarch Leona Helmsley." —LA READER

Thurs.-Sat. 8 pm / Sun. 7 pm • NOW THRU MAY 16th

New York
$2.95 • MARCH 29, 1993

LEONA GETS HER NAME IN L.A. LIGHTS

Leona Helmsley may be coming to Broadway.

The imprisoned hotel queen is the subject of a play opening later this month in Los Angeles. The producers are hoping to bring *Leona* to Broadway this fall after its eight-week run at L.A.'s Matrix Theatre.

Leona stars Joan Benedict, who is probably best known for her role as Edith Fairchild on *General Hospital*. The action takes place in a jail cell, according to spokesman Rob Wilcox, who adds that it's a sympathetic look at Helmsley, who is serving a prison term in the Danbury federal prison on tax-evasion charges. "It's a drama, but it's also warm and funny," says Wilcox. "She berates the man who brings her towels because they're not soft enough, but at times she shows warmth and compassion, especially in her love for Harry Helmsley."

JOAN BENEDICT IN *LEONA*

Something happens on stage—an epiphany—when you find that perfect role. Everything becomes clear. For me, *Leona* was that role. A number of friends and critics have referred to *Leona* as my finest hour ... or an hour and twenty minutes to be exact. I'm not sure if it is my best work; perhaps the best is still to come!

Other plays would follow in succeeding years including *The World Is Made of Glass* from novelist Morris West, *Lettice and Lovage* with Katharine Ross, *The Beauty Queen of Leenane*, *A Most Secret War,* and *The Vagina Monologues.* To date, I've done about forty plays and never once received a bad review.

Me appearing in the play Richard III

Words of encouragement from The World Is Made Of Glass *director Jeremiah Morris*

Left: Me with Lettice and Lovage *co-star Katharine Ross*

Me with Beauty Queen of Leenane *co-star Tyrone Power Jr.*

From the play A Most Secret War

As the *Collected Stories* run continued, I tried to encourage Jeremy and help rekindle his acting career. My agent got Jeremy an audition for the *My Name is Earl* television program and he nailed it. It would be his last performance. One day we were in the garden and he suddenly started

What The Critics Say About
JOAN BENEDICT

"THE AUDIT"
(by Emmy Award winner - Peter Lefcourt) "First wife, Myra - played sharply by Joan Benedict with tangible bitterness" (BACKSTAGE WEST - Ivy Brown)

"RICHARD III"
"Some of the actors stand out sharply. The latter includes Joan Benedict, the Duchess of York."
- T.H. McCulloh, DRAMA-LOGUE

"Joan Benedict's defiant Duchess of York (Richard's mother) enlivens a nest of squawking talons."
- Ray Loynd, LA TIMES

"Zealous performance..." - Drew Voros, DAILY VARIETY

"LEONA"
Joan Benedict is a vivid, compelling Leona Helmsley" - Polly Warfield
DRAMALOGUE

Joan Benedict gives a tour-de-force performance - sexy, gutsy yet somehow vulnerable - Michael Frym
L.A.READER

"THE WORLD IS MADE OF GLASS"
"Joan Benedict, the majestic actress, literally wipes all the other actors off the western map the moment she enters. She completely understands the style of the piece and makes it work beautifully. Benedict rivets us with her story of sexual deviance, murder and depravity lurking just below the elegant surface of Von Gamsfeld's monied and educated exterior."
-Travis Michael Holder, THE TOLUCAN

"Joan Benedict...Magda...Imperious...Seductive."
- Sylvie Drake, LOS ANGELES TIMES

"Benedict's enchanted, enchanting, victimized and victimizing Magda is a character capable of arousing pity and terror."
- Polly Warfield, DRAMA-LOGUE

"A MOST SECRET WAR"
Precise portrayal from Benedict.
- Elias Stimac, DRAMA-LOGUE

"THE MIND WITH THE DIRTY MAN"
Joan Benedict is enchanting as Don Knotts wife, sort of a wide-eyed Whitney Blake-Harriet Nelson role, suddenly stepping out and heating up.
- John C. Mahoney L.A. TIMES

"PROMISES, PROMISES"
Joan Benedict in her owl feathers is one of the comedy high points of the union plaza's "Promises, Promises".
Trudy Gillett, LAS VEGAS PANORAMA

Joan Benedict, a talented looker, does a memorable tipsy bit near how's finale.
Forrest Duke, VARIETY

Joan Benedict, has hilarious moments as a winsome tippler.
By John L. Scott, LOS ANGELES TIMES

"HELLO, I MUST BE GOING"
Icy ex-wife Ellen (Joan Benedict in the only focused performance of the night)
- Bill Raden, THEATRE

"PROMISES, PROMISES"
"Joan Benedict as Marge MacDougall is unbelievably good. She is talented, beautiful and totally smashed. Her scene with Chuck "A Fact Can Be" is a show stopper."
- Bernard Weiner, REGISTER

"Joan Benedict created a masterpiece out of the role of Marge MacDougall."
- John Yench
ANAHEIM BULLETIN

"Joan Benedict played a female souse to perfection."
- Ted Kree,
ORANGE COUNTY EVENING NEWS

"...Promises, Promises a rare review, especially Joan Benedict as the tipsy Marge MacDougall."
- Sondra Lowell
L.A. TIMES

"BEACHPLAY"
Joan Benedict confidently dispatches the flashiest role.
- Richard Scaffidi,
DRAMA-LOGUE

"WHERE NIGHTINGALES USED TO SING."
A heartfelt tribute to Tennessee Williams in which bag lady (Joan Benedict) fancies herself the reincarnation of Blanche du Bois. Benedict aims for the correct melancholy tone and collaborates well with Director Jan Marlyn
- Richard Scaffidi, DRAMA-LOGUE

"THE LOVE SONG OF ALEX VANDENBERG"
"Seasoned actress, Joan Benedict nearly upstaged Barr with genuine grace and gentility."
- by Jody Leader, DAILY NEWS CRITIC

expectorating. I rushed him to the hospital where he was diagnosed with esophageal cancer. They tried to operate but it was no use. The cause of death was listed as esophageal cancer with surgical complications. I had felt that Jeremy's excessive pot use may have contributed to his cancer. I loved him dearly and cared about him, and as our time together progressed, he was able to completely stop smoking on his own.

As with John and Rod, I remained with Jeremy during his entire hospital stay. None of my three guys ever complained during their final days. A number of hippies and Hells Angels showed up at his memorial service. Had Jeremy lived longer, I'm sure we would have gotten married. He called me his Ruby Lips …

Jeremy Slate

1926-2006

Only those who avoid love can avoid grief. The point is to learn from grief and remain vulnerable to love.

--John Brantner

Chapter 14

My Heart Will Go On

A FEW YEARS BACK I did a one woman play that I wrote called *The Loves of My Life*. The shows were sold out. It was essentially my life story. In it I talked about John, Rod and Jeremy and also sang fifteen songs! Fifteen songs? What was I thinking? It took a tremendous amount of courage to do that. I quickly developed a newfound admiration for singers. Remembering lyrics is hard if you're not a musician.

I loved all three of my guys. They were all so articulate and funny. I learned so much from each of them and they were always there for me. They were my champions. I always tried to encourage them. It was never a chore.

The Loves Of My Life *at the Gardenia in West Hollywood*

I always tell women to encourage their husbands. It makes for a good marriage. Relationships should be there to nurture and strengthen.

John, Rod, Jeremy

You need to have things in common. That's why I always preferred to be with someone in the arts. Oh, and never argue. It's a waste of time and quite destructive. I never once had an argument with any of my three guys. We were always having too much fun.

People often ask how I could have loved three different men. The fact is you can always find another love. It will be different, but it will be wonderful in its own way. Had it been up to me, I would have only been married once, for life. But I wasn't given that opportunity. I've never been to a therapist, but one evening I did have a conversation with one at a party. He couldn't understand why I was so happy after all I'd been through. I think it really just comes down to being a positive person.

Are people born with courage or a positive attitude? I don't know. I'm sure my childhood set me up to be able to handle the difficult situations that have come my way. I feel blessed to have had a positive outlook on life. I certainly feel far more fulfilled than sad. I never look for dark places, but always toward the light. For me, happiness is a choice. The memories I have

Steiger to receive award March 24

Joan Benedict Steiger

Joan Benedict Steiger will receive the Eternity Award at the Los Angeles Women's Theatre Festival March 24. Steiger has worked in theater, film and television. She has worked in television since its early days, appearing in everything from dramas to guest appearances. Steiger will be given the award at the gala opening night of the festival at the Electric Lodge, 1416 Electric Ave. in Venice, at 7 p.m.

At the Palm Beach International Film Festival with Ben Gazzara, Shohreh Aghdashloo and Michael Clarke Duncan

of my three guys are all happy ones. I simply don't allow myself to think negatively, but instead focus on the positive. I get tremendous joy out of living.

I have to ask myself, "What would my guys want me to be doing?" Would they want me to sit around and sulk or feel sorry for myself? No, they would want me to have a good life. They were all such great believers in me. They would want me to go on and continue on with this journey. And they would not want me to dwell on their deaths. Yes, these were tragedies, especially considering all the talent involved. But we who are still here have been given life, and we must live it to its fullest. And that's what my guys would want for me.

Me and my friends

My tap class

Me and my tap class instructor Joe Giamalva

Would I have changed anything? I don't think so. How could I have any regrets? What happened was beyond my control. Yes, my life has had its challenges, but one thing it hasn't been is boring, that's for sure. Even now, I can't wait to get up each morning to see what the day will bring. In fact, I love life so much I can hardly stand it! Life is just too fantastic to let it slip by, so take part in it! There is a reason why we're all here. And if you can find your purpose, you've succeeded!

It's so fun and exciting to be in this business. My father would have been proud that I became an actress. It's true . . . the industry's most successful actors have had the most difficult lives, which is not a coincidence. Those struggles are what give actors the necessary experiences they can draw on for their performances. I'll meet people who say, "Oh, maybe I'll give acting a try." I just want to slap them. You need training, you need experiences. It would be like me going up to a doctor and saying, "Oh, maybe I'll give hip replacement surgery a try."

Tap dance class keeps Malibuites on their toes

Photos by Cathryn Sack

Tap dance teacher Joe Giamalva's class begins with a basic warm-up: a simple shuffle on one foot for awhile, then the other, then circling the room behind the teacher, doing basic "flaps." As the hour-long class progresses, more steps are added until, almost surprisingly, they become an entire dance routine, with a flourishing finish.

Joan Steiger started tap dancing at age seven, but later hung up her shoes until a few years ago, when her late husband, Rod Steiger, urged her to take up dance again.

By Ward Lauren
Special to The Malibu Times

"Flap, flap, flap, ball-change, shuffle, hop step, flap, heel-drop!" Not just the unique percussive sounds but the words as well echo rhythmically from the fitness center at Zuma Beach Plaza three times a week as Malibu's adult tap dance class hoofs it up with veteran dancer and choreographer Joe Giamalva.

The class is drawing a growing number of women and yes, a man or two, to its Monday and Wednesday sessions. With seemingly unbridled enthusiasm they enjoy a three-phase participation in the venerable American dance form: learning the basic steps, performing them in a group dance routine, and, far from least, getting valuable pound-dropping cardiovascular exercise while having a whale of a good time.

Students have come to the Malibu class for a variety of reasons, none apparently having anything to do with serious hopes of future fame on the Broadway stage.

"The greatest joy of my life is tapping," said Malibu resident Joan Steiger, who first set foot to the dance floor at age seven. "You can never tap and not smile."

Although she has tap danced occasionally in television commercials, Steiger said she didn't have much time to practice her art during the years she and her late actor husband Rod Steiger traveled extensively. He urged her to take it up again when they settled in Malibu shortly before his death.

Hair stylist Bernie Safire, on the other hand, put on his first pair of tap shoes only eight months ago. An ex-gymnast, he occasionally works out on the trampoline and high bar to keep in shape, but now gets most of his physical conditioning in tap class.

"It's just about the most fun of anything I've ever done," Safire said enthusiastically. "People in the gym don't know what this is all about; this is great!"

Wini Rutter of Broad Beach, who also had never set foot into tap shoe until now, probably had bored the idea subconsciously for some 20 years, from the time a friend first told her about joining a tap class.

"I've always remembered how much she loved it," Rutter said. "I never thought about it for myself until I heard about this class, which I first thought would be a good way to enjoy aerobics. It is, and then Joe makes it so much fun I know just what my friend was talking about. I don't have any great goals in mind; it's just fun being in the class."

Giamalva's teaching method is strictly hands-on, or feet-on in this case, with liberal applications of fun

See **Tap dancing,** *page B*

Left: Floppers. Right: Puddin.

Kristen

I wanted this to be a fun, positive book and hopefully, I've achieved that goal. By the way, I'm currently single, so . . .

Epilogue

Mischievous

ANOTHER YEAR HAS COME TO AN END. I must be ancient! Funny, I don't feel ancient.

Writing about my life makes me happy. Since the time of my childhood, I have viewed each day as an adventure. My father was rarely home and my mother was always busy trying to navigate some business deal. Nevertheless, I enjoyed being me, either in the real world or in a make believe place.

One of the first books I ever read as a child was *Alice In Wonderland*. What a wonderful gift that was. Sometimes I would sit in the large sitting room at my grandfather's 7th Street home in Brooklyn and stare at the floor to ceiling mirrored wall and wonder what might be going on behind that mirror.

I remember a favorite picture of me taken when I was about seven years old. I'm sitting in my grandfather's lawn chair in the garden. In the photo I have this mischievous smile. I recall the picture with a great deal of love and affection. That was me . . . this is me. The look on my face in that photo has been indelibly ingrained in my soul.

That look is the way I approach life—always with a smile, and always with a delightful sense of mischief!

Thanks for the memories . . .

Sam Bobrick
Bill and Pat Daly
Tony and Patty Fantozzi
Ron and Val Friedman
James and Linda DeMetrick
Sebastian and Carmen Milito

Index

A
Academy Award x, xi, 10, 30, 36, 81, 102, 128, 133, 135, 136 142-144
Actor's Alley 98, 99
The Actor's Co-op 98
Adams, Don 94
Adler, Stella 98
Aghdashloo, Shohreh 196
The Ahmanson Theatre 97
Al Capone **125**, **126**, **127**, **130**
Alfred Hitchcock Presents 175
Alice 96
Alice in Wonderland 203
Allen, Steve 34, 35, 53, 107
Ambush Bay 89
American International Pictures 176
Anderson, Paul Thomas 102
Andrews, Julie 73

Anthony and Cleopatra 112
Apple Valley 80, 81, 84, 86
The Aquanauts (Malibu Run) 174
Arquette, Cliff 81, 84, 88
Arquette, David; Patricia; Rosanna 81
Ashford Castle 154
The Art Ford Show 36
Arthur, Bea 107
Astaire, Fred 4
Atkinson, Buddy 107
Atkinson, Stella 110
Audrey Rose 100, 101

B
Bacon, Kevin 100, 139
Bahia Mar Yacht Center 18
Ballet 4, 10
Ballintubber Abbey 153
Banderas, Antonio 142
Bardot, Bridget 37
Barger, Sonny 178
Bass, Newton T. 84, 86
Battaggia, Madame 10
Beatty, Warren x
The Beauty Queen of Leenane 186, 188
Belafonte, Harry 111
Belushi, John 32
Ben Hur 114
Bening, Annette 164
Bennett, Tony 162
Berenger, Tom 156, 160
Bernstein, Herman 66
The Best Years of Our Lives 41
The Beverly Hillbillies 107
Bewitched 178
The Big Knife 124
The Bionic Woman 96
Blair, Janet 115
Bloom, Claire 150
The Blue Mosque 149
The Blues Brothers 33
Bogart, Humphrey 47, 130, 133
Bonanza 176
The Botanical Gardens 4
The Bob Newhart Show 15
Body and Soul 140, 141
Boogie Nights 102

Born Losers 176, 177
Boxing 6, 21, 140
Bradbury, Ray 165
Brando, Marlon 128-130
Bridges, Lloyd 108
Brillstein, Bernie 32-34
Broadway 125, 173
Brolin, James 102
Brooklyn xiii, 1, 8, 203
The Brooklyn Academy of Music xiii, 6
Brooks, Mel 101
Brosnan, Pierce & Keely 152-154, 178
Brother "Gene" 8, 11-14, 22
Butterfield 8 43, 47, 96, 144

C
Cagney, James 41
California 23, 25, 26, 47, 93, 106, 119
Campbell, Glen 176, 177
Candid Camera 35, 36, 56, 58
Capitol 98, 99
Carnegie Hall 29
Carousel 53
Carter, Jimmy 167
Casey, William 30
Cash, Johnny 30
Cashman, Betty 29
Cassavetes, John 65
Cassidy, David 96
Cates, Gil 30
Cates, Joseph 30, 31
Cates, Phoebe 30
Cedars-Sinai Medical Center 119
Central Park 56
The Chase 41
The Chelsea Hotel xiv, 18-21
Chicago 57, 58, 63, 88
Chicago Sun-Times 58
Christie, Julie 136
Cinecitta Studios 30, 31
Clark, Ron & Sheila 110
Clary, Robert 91
Claudia 27, 28, 58, 74, 75, 85, 96, 102, 103, 145, 157
Clift, Brooks 42
Clift Hotel xi
Clift, Montgomery 42
Clinton, Bill 147

Clooney, George 111
Cochran, Steve 41, 42
Collected Stories xii, xiii, 183, 184, 189
Columbia 100
Combat 178
Connery, Sean 110
Conway, Tim 103, 104, 106, 107, 110
Corman, Roger 103
Crane, Bob 92
Crawford, Joan 47
Crazy in Alabama 142
Curtis, Tony 30, 124
The Cypress Inn 181

D
Daley, Richard 57
Davis Jr., Sammy 77, 110
Davison, Bruce 96
Day, Doris 181
Days of Our Lives 98
De Mille, Agnes 130
Dean, James 124
Deep Throat 100
Delon, Alain 151
Di Costanzo, Pasquale 10
Diller, Phyllis 93, 94
The Dirty Dozen 112
Donahue, Troy 15
Dorchester Hotel 121
The Doris Day Show 96
Dr. Faustus 3, 37
Dr. Kildare 175
Dr. Zhivago 136
Dreyfuss, Richard 152
Duncan, Micahel Clarke 196
Durgom & Katz 77
Durning, Charles 156
Dzundza, George 156

E
East of Eden 116
Eddy, Nelson 113
Eloise at the Plaza 4
ER 81
Evanview 77, 79, 108, 114
Everett, Chad 163

F

Fantasy Island 101
Farentino, James 156
Fast Times at Ridgemont High 30
Father xiv, 3, 6, 8, 9, 14, 17-22, 42, 92, 198, 203
FDR 47
Fellini 31
Fisher, Carrie 163
First National Touring Company 54, 70
Floppers 200
The Flying Dutchman (Frozen In Fear) 154
The Flying Nun 96
Fonda, Henry 94
Ford, Tony 31
Ford, Phil 81, 88
Forsythe, John 94
Fox 70
Funt, Allen 36, 56

G

Gable, Clark 29
Garland, Judy 47, 70
Garner, James 145, 157
Gazzara, Ben 196
Geary, Tony 98
General Hospital 97, 98
Get Smart 93
Ghostbusters 33
G.I. Blues 175
Giamalva, Joe 198
Girls! Girls! Girls! 174, 175
God Created Woman 37
Godfrey, Arthur 35
The Golden Fleecing 15, 16
The Good Soup 55
Gordon, Ruth 55
Graceland 182
Grand Guignol 42
Grandfather xiii, 1, 2, 203, 204
Grandmother 1
Granger, Red 80, 82-84
Grauman's Chinese Theatre 94
Grayson, Kathryn 43
Green, Walon 81
Gremlins 30
Griffin, Melanie 142
Griffith, Andy 109

Grimes, Tammy 178
Gunsmoke 176

H
Hagman, Larry 54
Hamilton, George 100
Hammerstein, Oscar 53
Happy Gilmore 33
The Happy Hooker Goes to Washington 100, 101
The Harder They Fall 130, 133, 140
Hare Krishnas 101
Have Gun, Will Travel 175
Hayes, Helen 29
Hayward, Leland 54
Heatherton, Joey 100
Hector Heathcoat 93
Hedren, Tippi 142
Hefner, Hugh 64
Helen of Troy 37
Hell's Angels '69 173, 176, 178
Hell's Belles 176
Henderson, Florence 54, 65, 66
Henson, Jim 33
Hepburn, Katharine 29, 112, 113
Herbie Rides Again 97
Heston, Charlton 113, 165
Hill Street Blues 81
History of the World, Part One 101
Hoffman, Dustin x
Hofstra College 23
Hogan's Heroes 90
Hollywood viii, xiv, 15, 33, 47, 77, 80, 85, 93, 94, 101, 112, 124, 126, 136, 139, 166, 183, 194
The Hollywood Sign 156, 159, 160, 166
Hollywood Squares 81
The Hollywood Walk of Fame 161
Honeymoon xi, 26, 148, 149
Hope, Bob 93-95, 115
Hopkins, Anthony 101
Hopkins, Miriam 173
Hopper, Dennis 176
Hopper, Hedda 70
Hotel 102
How to Succeed in Business Without Really Trying 93, 95, 110
Hunter, Jeffrey 93
Hunter, Tab 49
The Hurricane 140

I

I Dream of Jeanie 96
Idiot's Delight 97
In the Heat of the Night x, 133-135, 140, 142
The Incredible Hulk 101
Ingels, Marty 100
It Takes a Thief 96
Italian xii, xiii, 1, 2, 6, 10, 14, 31, 32, 39
Italy 1, 9-11, 31

J

Jewison, Norman 133, 135, 140, 142
The Jicky Club 31
Johnny Staccato 65
Johnston, Johnnie 43
Jones Beach 6, 14
Jones, Shirley 100, 130
Jones, Quincy 169
Just Beyond the Moon 176

K

Kanin, Garson 55, 97, 98
Kazan, Lainie 66
Keeler, Ruby 5
Kelly, Gene 30, 47
Kennedy, John F. 57, 62
The Kentucky Derby 152
The Kid 140
The King and I 53
Kirkland, Sally 155
Klemperer, Otto 91
Klemperer, Werner 91
Knotts, Don vii, 34, 103-107, 183
Kojak 101, 102
Kraft Theatre 36
Kristen 200
Kupcinet, Irv & Esther 58, 60, 63

L

La Mirada Theatre 106
Lamas, Fernando 44, 47
Lancaster, Burt 111
Landau, Martin 156
Larson, Keith 174
Las Vegas 74, 116
Laura 43
Law & Order 81

Lawnmower Man 178
Lawrence, Jennifer 111
Lee, Bill 73
Lee, Stan 163
Lemmon, Jack vii, 97, 107
Leona 183-186
Lettice and Lovage 186, 188
Lewis, Bobby 98
Linda Lovelace for President 100
Lindfors, Viveca 49
Lindsay, John 30
Linn, Bambi 130
Linkletter, Art 115
Lollobrigida, Gina 40, 94
Long Island 6, 22, 26, 28, 147
The Longest Day 112
Loren, Sophia 49
Los Angeles 26, 97, 122
Love, American Style 97
The Loves of My Life 193, 194
The Lunt-Fontanne Theatre 54

M
MacPhail School of Music 31
MacRae, Gordon 132
Malibu 47, 145-147
A Man for All Seasons 113
The Man from UNCLE 178
Mancini, Ray 141
Maness, Fred 43
Mann, Daniel 47, 96
Mannix 178
Margaret, Ann 166
Marguiles, Donald xii, 183
Marovitz, Abraham Lincoln 57, 61
Mars Attacks 153
Martin, Mary 54
Martin, Steve 30
Marvin, Lee 133
Mary Poppins 73
Mason, Marsha 101
Masquerade Party 44, 45, 123, 124
Mayo, Nick 115
McCormack, Pat 109
McDowell, Roddy 142
Meinch, George 22, 23, 25-28, 173
Meister, Barbara 68, 69

Memphis Mafia 77
Mepham High School 14, 16, 17
Merrick Middle School 14
Judge Merrick 146
MGM 47, 90
Miami High School 17, 18
Michaels, Lorne 33
Mickey 88, 89
Miller, Ann 5
Milito, Carmen 184
Milosevic, Milos 89
The Mind with the Dirty Man 105, 106
The Mini Skirt Mob 176
Mission: Impossible 178
Monroe, Marilyn 47
A Month of Sundays 155
Moore, Demi 100
Morris, Jeremiah 187
Morse, Robert 93, 95, 107
A Most Secret War 186, 189
Mother xiv, 1, 4-10, 12-14, 17, 18, 21-23, 25-29, 203
The Muppets 33
My Name Is Earl 189
Myhers, John vii, 15, 16, 21, 30-32, 35, 39, 40, 49-51, 53-59, 61, 63-75, 77, 79-82, 84-86, 88-98, 100-103, 106, 108-119, 121, 123, 136, 166, 182, 183, 191, 193, 195

N
The National Enquirer 144, 145
New York xiv, 2, 4, 10, 11, 13, 18-21, 25, 26, 29, 40, 47, 48, 56, 57, 74, 123, 136, 173
New York Daily News 3
New York Methodist Hospital 3
New World Pictures 103
Newman, Paul x
Normandy 22, 26, 173
NYPD Blue 81

O
O'Brian, Hugh 89
Octette Bridge Club 183
The Odd Couple 96
Oklahoma 53, 130, 132
On the Waterfront 128, 129
Onassis, Aristotle 1, 47
One Life to Live 178
Ozzie & Harriet 175

P
The Palm Beach International Film Festival 196
Paramount 178
Pare, Michael 155
Park Avenue 18, 22
Paris 13, 148
Parr, Jack 53
Parties viii, 14, 79, 94, 107-111, 152, 195
Patton 136
Pavarotti, Luciano 162
The Pawnbroker 130, 134, 170
Perry Mason 175
Pickford, Mary 29
Pitt, Brad 100, 111
Plaza Hotel 4
Pleshette, Suzanne 15, 16, 102
Plummer, Christopher 72, 73
Poitier, Sydney 133, 134
Police Story 178
Pollack, Kevin 156
Poston, Tom 15, 16, 34, 102, 107
Powell, Eleanor 5
Powell, Jane 74, 75
Power Jr., Tyrone 188
Presley, Elvis 77, 173, 174, 182
The Private Eyes 103
The Private Navy of Sgt, O"Farrell 93-95
The Prizefighter vii, 103-105
Promises, Promises 115-117
Prospect Park xiii, 1, 4
Puddin' 200

R
Radner, Gilda 33
Rainer, Luise 143
Rashomon 125
Reynolds, Burt 156, 158-160, 170
Richard III 186
Ripley, Robert 10
Ripley's Believe It or Not 10
Ritter, Tex 176
Robert Montgomery Presents 36
Roberts, Emma 156
Roberts, Eric 154-156
Roberts, Julia 156
Robinson-Duff, Francis 29
Robson, Mark 130

Rockefeller Center 28
Rockville Center 27
Rogers, Ginger 4, 5, 35
Rogers, Mimi 84, 85, 88, 156
Rogers, Richard 53-56, 61, 72
Rogers, Tristan 98
Rome xiii, 8-11, 31, 108, 148
Rome Opera Ballet School 10
Rooney, Mickey 70, 85, 88-90
Ross, Katharine 186, 188
Rossellini 31
Route 66 41, 175
Ryan, Meg 100
Ryan, Robert 111, 112

S
The Sand Pebbles 101
Santa Barbara 98
Sarandon, Susan 100
Saturday Night Bath in Apple Valley 80-84, 86-88
Saturday Night Live 32
Savalas, Telly 102
Schilling, Jerry 77, 78
Scott, George C. 136
Seven Brides for Seven Brothers 73
1776 100
The Shaggy D.A. 97
Shakespeare 112, 113
Shatner, William 102
Short, Martin 33
The Shrine Auditorium x
Sinatra, Frank 47, 162
The $64,000 Question 30, 31, 39
Slate, Jeremy 173-184, 189-193, 195
The Smith Family 94
The Sons of Katie Elder 175, 176
Sorvino, Mira xi
The Sound of Music 53-57, 61-74, 93, 115
Sousa, John Phillip 91
South Pacific 53, 73
Spencer, Rebecca xii
St. Paul Civic Opera 54
St. Savior's School 7, 8
Steiger, Anna 149, 150
Steiger, Rod ix-xii, 2, 45-47, 112, 123-171, 173, 182, 183, 191, 193, 195, 201
Streisand, Barbra 8
The Steve Allen Show 15, 33, 34

Strike It Rich 28
Stone, Sharon 156
Sunset Plaza vii, 77, 78, 79, 106
The Super Bowl 152

T
Tap dance 4, 9, 10, 116, 197-199
Tarzan 84, 178
Taylor, Elizabeth xi, xii, 40, 42, 43, 47, 48, 143-145
Temple, Shirley xi, 4
Teresa 128, 129
That Kind of Woman 49
Theatre Macabre 42
There Will Be Blood 102
This Could Be the Start of Something Big 34
Thomason, Barbara 89
Thompson, Kay 4
TJ Hooker 102
To Rome with Love 94
Tomei, Marisa 100
The Tonight Show 50, 53, 54
Tony Award 125
Top Hat 4, 5, 35
The Toronto Film Festival 142
Tracy, Spencer x
The Trials of Rosie O'Neill 142
True Grit 176
TWA 28, 29
21 Club 42, 47
The Twilight Zone 41

U
Universal 43
University of Rome 31
The Untouchables 41, 175

V
The Vagina Monologues 186
Vallee, Rudy 93, 110, 111
The Valley Music Theatre 113-115
Van Gogh, Vincent 148
The Venice Film Festival 151
Vines, Lee 43
The Virginian 176

W
Wagner, Robert 142

Walking Tall 100
Walters, Norby 156
The Waltons 96
Warner, Cy 115
Washington, Denzel 140
The Washington Post 3
Waterloo 131
Wayne, John 111, 176
W.C. Fields and Me 131
Weddings and Babies 49
West, Morris 186
West Point 16, 17
West Side Story 101
What's My Line? 43
White Heat 41
The Wild Bunch 81, 112
Willard 96
Williams, Bob 42
The William Morris Agency 31, 32, 34
Williams, Robin xi, xii
Win a Million Lire 31, 32
Winters, Jonathan vii, 93, 107, 109, 158
Wise, Robert 73, 101
The Wizard of Oz 143
The World Is Made of Glass 186, 187
World War II 22, 31
Wynn, Keenan 49, 50

Y
Yolie, Yole 10

About the Authors

Joan Benedict Steiger began her acting career as part of the original cast of *The Steve Allen Show* before becoming a regular on classic television programs including *Candid Camera* and *General Hospital*. Joan is also a star of the stage and screen and has appeared in numerous motion pictures including two with her late husband, Academy Award winner Rod Steiger.

In addition to co-authoring books with a *New York Times* best selling author, **David Minasian** has spent 30 years as an award winning writer, composer, producer and director working in the motion picture and music industries alongside many of Hollywood's top artists and filmmakers.

www.ingramcontent.com/pod-product-compliance
Lightning Source LLC
Chambersburg PA
CBHW071434150426
43191CB00008B/1123